Biography of a Runaway Slave

MIGUEL BARNET

Biography
of a
Runaway Slave

Translated by W. Nick Hill

CURBSTONE PRESS

Printed in the U.S. by BookCrafters
Cover design: Stone Graphics

Curbstone Press is a 501(c)(3) nonprofit publishing house whose operations
are supported in part by private donations and by grants from ADCO
Foundation, J. Walton Bissell Foundation, Inc., Witter Bynner Foundation
for Poetry, Inc., Connecticut Commission on the Arts, Connecticut Arts
Endowment Fund, Lannan Foundation, LEF Foundation, Lila Wallace-
Reader's Digest Literary Publishers Marketing Development Program,
administered by the Council of Literary Magazines and Presses, The Andrew
W. Mellon Foundation, National Endowment for the Arts, and The
Plumsock Fund.

Library of Congress Cataloging-in-Publication Data

Montejo, Esteban, b. 1860.
    [Biografía de un cimarrón. English]
    Biography of a runaway slave : a novel / [edited] by Miguel Barnet ;
translated by W. Nick Hill.
      p. cm.
    Previously published: The autobiography of a runaway slave / edited by
Miguel Barnet ; translated from the Spanish by Jocasta Innes. 1st American
ed. New York : Pantheon Books, 1968.
    ISBN 1-880684-18-7 : $11.95
    1. Montejo, Esteban, b. 1860. 2. Fugitive slaves—Cuba—Biography. 3.
Revolutionaries—Cuba—Biography. 4. Cuba—History—Revolution,
1895-1898—Personal narratives. 5. Plantation life—Cuba—History—19th
century. I. Barnet, Miguel, 1940- . II. Hill, W. Nick, 1944- . III.
Title.
CT518.M6A3313   1994
863-dc20   94-12832

distributed by
InBook
Box 120261
East Haven, CT 06512

published by
CURBSTONE PRESS
321 Jackson Street
Willimantic, CT 06226

CONTENTS

Biography of a
Runaway Slave

Translator's Preface

In the early years of the Cuban Revolution, the encounter between two men from very different backgrounds, a writer and an illiterate former slave, produced the story of a remarkable life. It was not a chance encounter. Because he was interested in Afro-Cuban religions, Miguel Barnet, an anthropologist/writer, followed up on an article he had seen in the paper about a nursing home, some of whose residents were over 100 years old. Esteban Montejo was 103 in 1963 when Barnet first began to interview him. What increasingly intrigued the anthropologist was the uniqueness of Montejo's life: a young slave on a sugar plantation, who ran away to live as a maroon in the woods, who fought in the War of Independence (1895-1898), who worked as a wage laborer after the war, who witnessed the takeover of Cuba by U.S. troops and, finally, as an old man who finds meaning and purpose in the Cuban Revolution. What Barnet understood as well was that the careful recording of interviews with Montejo using established ethnographic field practices could produce a document that told the unvarnished story of "an authentic actor in the process of history in Cuba." Montejo's was a life story that could speak for a collective sense of the whole of Cuban society.

In the "Introduction" to the first edition of *Biografía de un cimarrón* (1966), from which the above quote comes, Barnet makes the following disclaimer: "I know that to ask an informant to speak is, in a certain sense, to make literature.

But I did not intend to create a literary text, a novel." Written before the Casa de las Américas literary award recognized the category of "literatura testimonial," Barnet's insistence on the "objective" and realist nature of recreating Montejo's story in language makes perfect sense as an antidote to merely "fictionalizing" a man's life. But Barnet also phrased the story in the modulated first person voice of autobiography, and by so doing he early on staked out the broad dimensions of the theoretical debates that have since taken place over the complex dynamics of literature's relationship to history with regard to giving voice to the oppressed.

The first English translation of Montejo's story took as its title *Autobiography of a Runaway Slave* (U.S. Edition, 1968) in recognition of its formal structure, but in so doing it failed to recognize the complex process of reproducing the text. The current translation goes back to the original title of *Biography*, with the understanding that the title, like the text itself, needs to be analyzed in the act of reading. "Biography" invites the reader to become involved in the process of hearing and deciphering the multiple voices in the story: the cimarrón Esteban, the "gestor/ writer" Miguel Barnet, and now an "invisible" translator.

The change in title for this seemingly monovocal text prompts questions about translation that also bear on the nature of the story and how it was told. After all, what Barnet attempts to create is an awareness of the process of giving voice to Esteban Montejo without making it an invented or "folkloric" voice. It should be Montejo/Barnet's voice that speaks a whole people, and marks a whole epoch, an I that speaks a we. It is this sense of responsibility in creation that links aesthetics and history so intimately in this story. Is the role of the translator easily understood to be akin to Barnet's role in giving order and printed words to

Montejo's life story? Is there a relationship between the "editor" Barnet and the translator analogous to the relationship that existed between Barnet, Montejo and Cuba?

If so, my responsibilities are double, like those of the biographer, who is true to the subject. And they are like those of the translator, who is true to the original in the more traditional sense. My challenge or burden as translator is to provide or suggest the sounds that come most directly from Montejo himself, the "aroma" of the original as Claribel Alegría has put it. To the extent that I fail, the loss is sadly more than mine alone but my responsibility alone.

In the "Post Scriptum" to the 1987 Argentine edition of *Biography*, Barnet says of Esteban Montejo: "He died the 10th of February 1973 at 113 years of age. That same year marks the 100th anniversary of the Abolition of slavery in Cuba and also in the Americas, since Cuba was the last country to overcome this affront to the human condition. With the present edition, I want to pay a modest personal homage to that action, which was taken not by grace of the powers that be, but rather was a victory won by the oppressed, by the slaves."

W. Nick Hill

SLAVERY

First Memories

There are things in life I do not understand. Everything about Nature seems obscure to me, and the gods even more. They're the ones who are supposed to give birth to all those things that a person sees, that I seen, and that do exist for sure. The gods are willful and ornery. That's why so many strange things have gone on around here. I remember from before, during slavery, I spent a lot of time looking upwards because I've always really liked the sky—it's so full of color. One time the sky turned into a glowing ember, and there was a terrible drought. Another time there was an eclipse of the sun. It began at four in the afternoon and was seen all over the island. The moon seemed to be fighting with the sun. I began to realize everything was going backwards. It was getting darker and darker and then lighter and lighter. The chickens perched on the tops of posts. Folks were so scared they couldn't talk. Some died of heart attacks, and some were struck dumb.

I seen the same thing other times but in a different place. And I wouldn't ask why it happened for anything in the world. The long and short of it is that I know everything depends on Nature. Nature is everything. Even what you can't see. And we men can't do those kinds of things because we're subjects of a God—Jesus Christ is the one most talked about. Jesus Christ was not born in Africa. He came direct from Nature herself because Mary was a virgin. The strongest gods are the ones from Africa. I tell you it's a fact they could fly. And they did whatever they wanted with their hexes. I don't know how they allowed slavery. Truth is that I set myself to thinking about it, and I can't get it. In my opinion it all began with the red kerchiefs. The day they crossed over the wall. The wall was very old in Africa and went along the whole coast. It was a wall made out of palm fronds and wicked bugs that bit like the devil They scared off the whites who were trying to get into Africa for many years. But it was the color scarlet that ruined all of them. And the kings and all the rest surrendered to it like nothing at all.

When the kings saw the white men, I think it was the Portuguese who were the first, pull out their red kerchiefs as if they were waving hello, they said to the blacks: "Go get one of those scarlet cloths, go on." And the blacks, excited by the red, ran like little lambs to the boats, and they were caught right there. Black men have always really liked red. That color is to blame for putting chains on them and sending them to Cuba. And then they couldn't return to their homeland. That's the reason there was slavery in Cuba. When the English discovered that business, they wouldn't allow more blacks to be brought, and then slavery ended and that other part began, the free part. It was around the 80s.

For me, none of that is forgotten. I lived through it all. I even remember my godparents told me the date I was born. It was the 26th of December, 1860, San Esteban's day, the one on the calendar. That's why my name is Esteban. My family name is Montejo, for my mother, who was a slave of French origin. My middle name is Mera. But that one hardly anyone knows about. Anyway it's not right, so why use it? My real middle name is Mesa. What happened was that they put it down wrong in the records, and I left it that way. Since I wanted to have two names like everybody else, so I wouldn't be called "jungle baby," I took that one, and there it was. The name Mesa came from a certain Pancho Mesa in Rodrigo. That seems reasonable since he raised me after my birth. He was my mother's master. Of course, I never seen him, but I know the story is true because my godparents told it to me. And I've never forgotten anything they ever told me.

My godfather was named Gin Congo,[1] and my godmother, Susana. I was to get to know them around the 90s, when the war hadn't yet really started up. An old black man who was at the same mill they were, and who knew me, gave me details about them. He himself took me to see them. I gradually got into the habit of visiting them in Chinchilla, the district where they lived, near Sagua la Grande. Since I didn't know my parents, I asked about them first. Then I learned about their names and other details. They even told me the plantation where I was born. My father's name was Nazario, and he was Lucumí from Oyó. My mother, Emilia Montejo. They also told me my parents had died in Sagua. Truth is that I would have liked to meet them, but because I saved my skin, I was unable to. If I had come out of the woods, they would have caught me on the spot.

Because I was a runaway slave, I never met my parents. I never ever seen them. But what is true can't be sad.

Like all children of slavery, the criollitos, as they were called, I was born in the infirmary where they took the pregnant black women to give birth. I think it was at the Santa Teresa plantation, though I'm not real sure. What I do remember is that my godparents talked to me a lot about that plantation and its owners, people by the name of La Ronda. That's the name my godparents had for a long time, until slavery left Cuba.

Blacks were sold like piglets, and they sold me right off— that's why I don't remember anything about that place. I do know that the plantation was near where I was born, which is in that northern region of Las Villas, Zulueta, Remedios, Caibarién, all those towns on down to the ocean. Then the picture of another plantation comes to mind, Flor de Sagua. I don't know if that's the place where I worked for the first time. What I am sure about is that I ran away from there once. I rebelled, by God, and I ran away. Who wanted to work! But they caught me like a little lamb, and they put some shackles on me that I can still feel if I really think about it. They tied them on me tight and put me to work and all of that. You talk about this kind of thing now and folks don't believe you. But I experienced it, and now I've got to talk about it.

The owner of that plantation had one of those long strange, connected names. He was a million bad things, a blockhead, grouchy, stuffy...He drove around through the cane fields in the carriage with his buddies and his wife. He would wave with his kerchief, but he wouldn't come up close on a bet. The masters never went into the fields. This one's case was strange. I remember he had an elegant black, a first-rate driver, with an earring and all. All those coachmen were ass-kissers and snitches. They were what you call colored dandies.

At Flor de Sagua I first began work with the wagons carrying bagazo. I would sit in the driver's seat and steer the mule. If the wagon was very full I would stop, get down, and lead him by the reins. The mules were stubborn, and you had to pull them very hard. Your back would start to get humped. A lot of those folks walking around sort of humped over is because of those mules. The wagons went out full, right up to the top. They were always unloaded in the batey, and you had to spread out the bagazo to dry. You pulled the bagazo down with a hook. Then you took it bunched up and dry to the ovens. That was done to get the steam up. I think it was the first job I had. That's what my memory tells me anyway.

All the parts inside the mill were primitive. Not like today, with lights and fast machinery. They were called cachimbos because that word meant a tiny mill. In those cachimbos, cane sugar was made into muscovado. There were some mills that didn't make sugar, just molasses and raspadura. Almost all those mills had a single owners and were known as trapiches. In the cachimbos there were three kettles. The kettles were big, made out of copper and wide mouthed. In one, the raw cane juice was cooked, in another the cachaza was beaten, and in the third the cane syrup reached the graining point. We called cachaza what was left of the cane juice. It came out like a hard crust that was healthy food for the pigs. After the cane syrup was ready, you took a trough, and with a big ladle attached to a stick, you poured the syrup into the trough, and from there to the crystallizing pan which was standing a short ways from the boiler. There the muscovado set up, which was the unrefined sugar. The best part of the molasses remained in it. In those days that thing you call a centrifuge didn't exist.

Once the fresh sugar was in the cooling room, you had to go in there barefoot, with a pick and a shovel and a hand barrow. One black always went in front and another behind. That hand barrow was to carry the hogsheads to the draining room, a large depository with two boards where the barrels were placed so that the sugar would drain. The molasses that leaked out of the barrel went to the batey and was fed to the sheep and the piglets. It fattened them up right quick.

To make refined sugar there were some big funnels where the muscovado was put to be refined. That sugar was like sugar nowadays, like white sugar. The funnels were known as molds.

I know this part of making sugar better than most folks, who only knew about the cane out in the fields. And to tell the truth, I prefer the inside work, because it's more comfortable. In Flor de Sagua I worked in the cachimbo's cooling room. But that's after I was experienced with the bagazo. That was a pick and shovel job. To my mind, even cutting cane was better. I must have been about ten, and that's why they didn't send me to the fields. But ten years of age then was like saying thirty now because children worked like oxen.

If a little black boy was pretty and lively, they sent him inside, to the master's house. There they began to sweeten him up, and...what do I know! The fact is that the little black boy had to spend his time shooing flies because the masters ate a lot. And they put the little boy at the head of the table while they ate. They gave him a big long fan made of a palm frond. And they told him: "Shoo, so those flies don't fall in the food!" If a fly fell on a plate,they scolded him severely and even whipped him. I never did this work because I never liked to be near the masters. I was a cimarrón from birth.

Life in the Barracoons

All the slaves lived in barracoons.[2] Those living quarters are gone now so nobody can see them. But I seen them, and I never had a good thought about them. The masters sure did say that barracoons were little boxes of gold. The slaves didn't like living in those conditions because being closed-in suffocated them. The barracoons were big although there were some mills that had small ones. It depended on the number of slaves in the work force. About two hundred slaves of all different colors lived at Flor de Sagua. The barracoon was in the form of two rows that faced each other, with a big door in the middle and a thick padlock that locked the slaves in at night. There were barracoons made of wood and others made of cement with tiled roofs. Both kinds had a dirt floor and were filthy as hell. There certainly was no modern kind of ventilation inside. A little hole in the wall of the room or a little tiny window with bars was all there was. So the place swarmed with fleas and ticks that gave the entire work force infections and sickness. Those ticks were witches. And so the only thing to get rid of them was hot lard, and sometimes even that didn't work. The masters wanted the barracoons to look clean outside so they painted them with whitewash. The blacks themselves were given that task. The master would say to them: "Get some whitewash and spread it evenly." The whitewash was prepared in big buckets in the barracoons, in the central patio.

Horses and goats didn't go into the barracoons, but there was always some fool dog sniffing around looking for

Condition

food. People had to stay in the rooms of the barracoons, which were small and hot. Rooms! In reality they were furnaces. They had doors with latch keys so nobody would get robbed. But watch out for the little criollos who were born rascally, with a thieving instinct. They would get out from under the covers at night to go around stealing like the dickens.

In the center of the barracoons, the women washed their husband's clothes, their children's, and their own. They washed in washtubs. Washtubs during slavery weren't like the ones today. Those then were more rustic. And you had to take them to the river so they would swell up to hold water because they were made of codfish boxes, the big ones.

Outside the barracoon there weren't any trees, nor inside either. The barracoon was bare dirt, empty, and lonely. A black man couldn't get used to that. Blacks like trees, woods. Maybe the Chinese could! Africa was full of trees, ceibas, cedars, banyon trees. Not China. Over there they had plants that grew along the ground, creepers, purslane, morning glories...Since the rooms were tiny, the slaves did their business in a latrine, as they called it. It was in a corner of the barracoon. That's a place everybody went to. And to dry your fotingo, afterwards, you had to use plants like feverfew and corn cobs.

The mill's bell was at the gateway.[3] It was struck by the assistant overseer. At four-thirty in the morning they rang the Ave María. I think there were nine strokes. You had to get up right away. At six in the morning they struck another bell which was the line-up bell, and you had to form up on the dirt in front of the barracoon. The men on one side and the women on the other. Then into the fields until eleven in the morning, when we ate beef jerky, 'taters, and bread.

Then, at sunset, came the prayer bell. At eight-thirty they rang the last bell for bed. It was called silence.[4]

The assistant overseer slept in the barracoon and kept watch. In the batey there was a white nightwatchman, a Spaniard, who kept guard. Everything was based on leather and vigilance. After some time had passed, and the slaves' clothing was worn out, they would give the men a new set made of Russian cloth or canvas, a thick fabric, good for the fields. Tambor, which were field pants with big open pockets, a shirt, and a wool cap for the cold. Shoes were generally rawhide, low-cut, with two straps to tie them. The old men wore house slippers or chacualas, which had a flat sole with a thong for the big toe. That has always been an African style though now whites wear them and call them slippers or mules. The women were issued a blouse, a skirt, a petticoat, and when they had a conuco, a small garden, they themselves bought the kind of white petticoats that were prettier and stylish. They wore gold or pearl earrings in their ears. Those items could be bought from the Moors or Turks who came right up to the barracoons once in a while. They carried boxes slung from their shoulders on a thick leather strap.

Lottery ticket vendors also got into the barracoons. They cheated the blacks, selling them the highest priced tickets, and when a ticket came out a winner, they never showed up again. The guajiros came around to trade milk for beef jerky. They sold it for four centavos a bottle. Blacks bought it because the master didn't supply milk. Milk cures infections and cleans you out. That's why you had to drink it.

But it was the small gardens that saved many slaves. They provided them real nourishment. Almost all the slaves had their conucos. They were little strips of dirt for gardening. They were real close to the barracoons, almost right in back.

They grew everything there: sweet potato, squash, okra, corn, peas, horse beans, beans like limas, limes, yuca and peanuts. They also raised piglets. And so those products were sold to the guajiros who came straight from town. Truth is that the blacks were honest. Since they didn't know much yet, being honest just came naturally. They sold their things very cheap. Full grown pigs were worth an ounce or one and a half ounces in gold, which was the money back then. But they never liked to sell their 'taters. I learned from the old timers to eat 'taters, which are very nutritious. During slavery the main thing was pig meat. They were given 'taters for food Pigs at that time produced more lard than they do nowadays. I think it's because they lived a more natural life. You had to let the pig to wallow around in the pig sty. That lard of theirs was sold in ten kilo batches. Every week the guajiros would come for their supply. They always paid in silver half pesos. Later on, that coin dropped to a quarter, or half a half. The centavo was unknown because Alfonso XII hadn't been crowned yet. It was after the coronation that the centavo came. King Alfonso wanted to change even the money. The copper calderilla, which I think was worth two cents, came to Cuba with other new money on account of the King.

Strange as it may seem, blacks had fun in the barracoons. They had their pastimes and their games. There were also games in the taverns, but those were different. One of the ones they played the most in the barracoons was tejo. You put a corn cob, split in half, on the ground. You placed a coin on top of it. You drew a line on the ground a short distance away, and you threw a stone from the line toward the corn cob. If the stone hit the corn cob, and the coin fell on the stone, the man took the coin as his. If it fell close to the corn cob, no coin. Tejo caused great disputes. In such cases, you had to measure with a straw to see if the coin was closer to the player than to the corn cob.

That game was played in the patio like the game of bowling. But bowling wasn't played much. I seen it no more than two or three times. There were some black coopers who made the sticks in the shape of bottles and the wooden balls for playing. It was an open game, and everybody could join in. Except for the Chinese, who were pretty standoffish. You rolled the balls along the flat ground to try to knock down the four or five sticks at the other end. It was the same game as the one that's played today in the city, but the difference is that with the older one, there were fights over the bets. That surely didn't please the masters. That's why they prohibited some games, and you had to play them when the overseer wasn't looking. The overseer was the one who told the news, news and gossip.

The game of mayombe was linked to religion. Even the overseers got involved, hoping to benefit. They believed in ghosts so that's why no one today should be surprised that whites also believe in those things. You played mayombe with drums. You put a nganga or big pot in the middle of the patio.

All the powers, the saints, were in that cazuela And mayombe was a useful game, but the saints had to be present. The players began to play the drums and to sing. They brought things for the ngangas. The blacks asked about their health, and their brothers' and sisters' health, and asked for harmony among them. They did enkangues which were hexes made with dirt from the cemetery. With that dirt you made four corners in little mounds to resemble the points of the universe. They put star-shake, which was an herb, in the pot with corn straw to hold human beings. When the master punished a slave, all the others picked up a little dirt and put it in the pot. With that dirt they were abut to bring about what they wanted. And the master fell ill or some harm came to his family because while the dirt was in the pot, the master was a prisoner in there, and not even the devil could get him out. That was the Congo people's revenge on the master.

There were taverns close to the mill. There were more taverns than ticks in the woods. They were a kind of a small general store where you could buy everything. The slaves themselves traded in the taverns. They sold beef jerky that they stored up in the barracoons. During the day and sometimes even in the evening, the slaves could go to the taverns. But that didn't happen at all the plantations. There was always some master who wouldn't give permission for his slaves to go. The blacks went to the taverns for rum. They drank a lot to keep their strength. A shot of good rum cost a half peso. The owners drank a lot of rum, too, and I can't begin to tell you about all the to-do there was. Some of the tavern keepers were old men retired from the Spanish army who got a little pension, some five or six pesos.

The taverns were made of wood and yagua palm fronds. None of that cement you see in stores nowadays. You had to sit on piles of jute sacks, or else stand up. In the taverns they sold rice, beef jerky, lard, and all kinds of beans. I seen hard-case tavern owners who cheated the slaves by charging them fat prices. I seen brawls where a black was beaten up and couldn't return to the tavern. In booklets they noted down all the purchases, and when a slave spent a half peso, they put down one mark, and when he spent two, two marks. That's how the system worked for buying everything else, the flour cookies, round and sweet, salt biscuits, different colored sweets the size of chickpeas made of flour, water bread, and lard. The water bread cost a half peso a loaf. It was different from the water bread today. I preferred that older kind. I also remember that they sold some candy called capricho, made of white flour, sesame seeds and peanuts. Sesame seeds, you know, were a Chinese thing because their salesmen went around the plantations selling them. Those Chinese peddlers were old indentured workers who couldn't lift up their arms to cut cane any longer, so they started selling things.

The taverns were smelly. They got that strong smell from the goods hanging from the beams, sausages, hams curing, and red mortadella. Even so, it was where you could fool around to relax. Men spent all their time in that silliness Black men really wanted to be good in games. I recall a game they called "the cracker." The way that game worked was that four or five hard salt crackers were placed on the wooden counter or any board, and the men had to hit the crackers hard with their dicks to see who could break the crackers. The one who broke the crackers won. That game attracted betting and drinking. Blacks as well as whites played it.

Another pastime was the jug game. They would take a big jug with a hole in the top and stick their do-hickey through it. The one who reached the bottom was the winner. The bottom was covered with a little layer of ash so that when the man took his dick out it was easy to see if he had touched bottom or not.

They played other games too, like cards. It's best to play cards with oil-coated cards, which are the right ones to use. There were many kinds of card games. Some liked to play face cards, others mico where you could win a lot, but I preferred monte, which started first in private homes and then spread to the countryside. During slavery, monte was played in the taverns and in the masters' houses. But I picked it up after Abolition. Monte is very complicated. You have to put two cards on the table and guess which of those two is higher than the three you keep in you hand. It was always played for money, and that was its attraction. The banker was the one who dealt the cards, and the players bet. You could win a lot. I won money every day. The truth is that monte was my vice. Monte and women. And not for nothing because you would have to look around a lot for a better player than me. Each card had its own name. Like nowadays, but it so happens that cards nowadays are not as colorful. In my day, there were queens, jacks, kings, aces, and then came the numbers from two to seven. The cards had pictures of men on them with crowns or on horseback. You could easily see they were Spaniards because those types with the lace collars and long hair never existed in Cuba. What was here before were Indians.

Sundays were the noisiest days on the plantation. I don't know where the slaves found the energy. The biggest fiestas during slavery took place on that day of the week. There were plantations where the drum began at noon or at one. At Flor de Sagua it started very early. At sunrise the noise began, and the games, and the children began to spin around. The barracoon came to life in a flash. It seemed like the world would come to an end. And, even with all the work, everybody got up happy. The overseer and his assistant came into the barracoon and started fooling around with the women. I noticed that the ones who were least involved were the Chinese. Those bastards didn't have an ear for the drums. They were standoffish. It was that they thought a lot. In my opinion they thought more than the blacks. Nobody paid them any mind. And folks just went on with their dances.

The one I remember best is the yuka. In the yuka three drums were played: la caja, la mula and the cachimbo, which was the littlest. Behind the drums someone played two hollowed-out cedar trunks with two sticks. The slaves themselves made them, and I think they called them catá. Yuka was danced in pairs, and the movements were dramatic. Sometimes they swooped like birds, and it even seemed like they were going to fly they moved so fast. They did little jumps with their hands on their hips. Everybody sang to encourage the dancers.

There was another more complicated dance. I don't know if it was a dance or a game because the punches given out were serious. That dance was called the maní. The maní dancers made a circle of forty or fifty men. And they began to slap at each other. The one who got hit went out to dance. They wore ordinary work clothes and put red kerchiefs with drawings on them around their heads and waists. Those kerchiefs were used to tie up the slaves' clothes to take them to be washed. They were known as vayajá or red-checkered kerchiefs. So that the licks of the maní would be the most painful kind, their wrists were charged up with any old kind of witchcraft. The women didn't dance but made a hand-clapping chorus. They would shout from the scare they got because sometimes a black would fall down and never get up again. The maní was a cruel game. The dancers didn't bet on the challenges. At some plantations, the masters themselves bet, but at Flor de Sagua I don't remember them doing it. What the masters did do was to prohibit the blacks from hitting each other too much because sometimes they got so beaten up they couldn't work. Boys couldn't play, but they took it all in. Take me, for example, I will never forget it.

Every time the announcing drum started up, the blacks would go down to the creek to bathe. Near every mill was a little creek. There were cases where a woman waited behind and met a man as he went into the water. Then they fooled around and began to do their business. Or, if not that, they went to the reservoirs, which were pools at the mill made to store water. They played hide and seek there, and the men chased the women to have sex with them.

The women who didn't play that little game stayed in the barracoon and took a bath in a washtub. Those tubs were big, and there were only one or two for the entire work force.

Men's shaving and haircutting was done by the slaves themselves. They took a big knife, and like you trim a horse, that's how they cut the kinks out of a black's hair. There was always someone who liked to cut hair, and he was the most experienced. He trimmed the way they do it today. And it never hurt because hair is the strangest thing—even though you see it grow and all, it's dead. Women combed their hair in curls in little rows. Their heads would look like Castilian melons. They liked that busy work of combing their hair one way one day and another way the next. One day with rows, another with curls, another, conked. To clean your teeth you used soap-tree bristles that left them very white. All that fuss was for Sundays.

On that day, each and every person had his special outfit. The blacks used to buy rawhide boots I haven't seen since. They would buy them in nearby stores, the ones they could go to with the master's permission. They wore kerchiefs of vayajá red and green around their necks. They wore them on their heads and around their waists like in the maní dance. They also put on earrings, and gold rings on every finger. Pure gold. Some didn't wear gold but had silver bracelets all the way to their elbows. And patent leather shoes.

Slaves of French descent danced in pairs, at arm's length. They did slow turns. If there was an outstanding dancer, silk kerchiefs were tied around his leg. Of all colors. That was the prize. They sang in patois and played two big drums with their hands. It was called "The French Dance."

I knew about an instrument that was called the marímbula, and it was tiny. They made it with wicker, and it had a deep sound like a drum. It had a hole where the sound came out. With that marímbula they accompanied the Congo drums, and maybe the French drums, but I can't remember. The marímbulas sound very strange, and many people, mostly the guajiros, didn't like them because they said they were voices from beyond the grave.

As I understand it, at that time the guajiros made music using only a guitar. Later, around the year 1890, they played danzones on those pianolas with accordions and gourds. But the white man has always had music different from the black. White man's music has no drum at all. Tasteless.

The same thing more or less happens with religions. The African gods are different although they seem to resemble the other ones, the gods of the priests, which are stronger and less decorated. Right now, if you up and go to a Catholic church, you see no apples, no rocks, no rooster feathers. But in an African household those are the first things you see. The African is more down to earth.

I knew about two African religions in the barracoons, the Lucumí and the Conga. The Conga was the more important. At Flor de Sagua it was well known because the witches put spells on people. They gained the trust of all the slaves with their fortune-telling. I came to know the older blacks more after Abolition.

But at Flor de Sagua I remember the chicherekú. The chicherekú was a little Congo man. He didn't speak Spanish.

religion
cathdecism vs. African

He was a small man with a big head who went running
through the barracoons. He would jump up and land on
your back. I seen it many times. I heard him squeal like a
guinea pig. That's a fact, and even in the Porfuerza
sugarmill, up to a few years ago, there was one who ran
around that way. People used to run away from him because
they said he was the devil himself and was allied with
mayombe and with death. You couldn't play with
chicherekú because it was dangerous. As for me, in truth, I
don't like to talk much about him because I haven't seen him
again, and if by happenstance...well, devil take it!

For the work of the Congo religion they used the dead
and animals. They called the dead nkise and snakes majases,
or emboba. They prepared cazuelas and everything, and
that's where the secret to make hexes was. They were called
ngangas. All the Congos had their ngangas for mayombe.
The ngangas had to work with the sun. Because he has
always been the intelligence and the strength of men. As the
moon is for women. But the sun is more important because
he gives life to the moon. The Congos worked with the sun
almost every day. When they had a problem with some
person, they followed that person along any path and
gathered up the dirt they walked on. They saved it and put
it in the nganga or in a secret little corner. As the sun went
down, the life of the person would leave him. And at sunset
the person was quite dead. I say this because it happens that I
seen it a lot during slave times.

If you think about it, the Congos were murderers. But if
they killed someone, it was because some harm was being
done to them, too. No one ever tried to work a hex on me
because I have always been a loner, and I've never cared to
know too much about other people's business.

Witchcraft is more common with the Congos than with the Lucumís. The Lucumís are more allied to the Saints and to God. They liked to get up early with the strength of the morning and look at the sky and pray and sprinkle water on the ground. When you least expect it, the Lucumí is doing his work. I have seen old blacks kneeling on the ground for more than three hours speaking in their tongue and telling the future. The difference between the Congo and the Lucumí is that the Congo does things, and the Lucumí tells the future. He knows everything through the diloggunes, which are snails from Africa. With mystery inside. They're white and a little lumpy. Eleggua's eyes are made from that snail. *Lucumís*

The old Lucumís would lock themselves in the rooms of the barracoon, and they would clean the evil a person had done out of him. If there was some black man who had desire for a woman, the Lucumí would calm him down. I think they did that with coconuts, obi, which were sacred. They are the same as the coconuts today, which are still sacred and can't be touched. If someone dirtied the coconut, he would get a severe punishment. I always knew when things were going good because the coconut said so. He ordered Alafia to be pronounced so everyone would know there was no tragedy. All the saints spoke through the coconuts. Now the master of all of them was Obatalá. Obatalá was an ancient, so I heard, who was always dressed in white. They said that Obatalá was the one who created you, and who knows what else. People come from Nature, and so does Obatalá.

The old Lucumís liked to have their figurines, their gods, made of wood. They kept them in the barracoon. All those figurines had a big head. They were called oché. The

Eleggua was made of cement, but Changó and Yemayá were made of wood, and the carpenters made them themselves.

On the walls of the rooms they made marks of the saints with charcoal and whitewash. They were long lines and circles. Even though each was a saint, they said the marks were secret. Those blacks kept everything a secret. Today they've changed a lot, but back then, the hardest thing in the world was to get them to trust you.

The other religion was Catholicism. It was introduced by the priests who wouldn't go into the barracoons during slavery for love or money. The priests were very neat and tidy. They had a serious look that didn't sit well in the barracoons. They were so serious that there were even blacks who hung on their every word and obeyed them to the letter. They learned the catechism, and then they would read it to the others. With all the words and the prayers. Those were the house slaves, and they met with the other slaves, the field slaves, in the bateyes. They came to be the priests' messengers. Truth is, I never learned that doctrine because I did not understand it at all. I don't think the house slaves did either but because they were so refined and so well-treated, they became Christians. The household slaves got consideration from the masters. I never seen a severe punishment for a one of them. When they were sent to the fields to cut cane or take care of the pigs, they pretended to be sick and didn't work. That's why field slaves didn't want to see them at all, not even in a painting. Sometimes they went to the barracoon to visit with a family member. And they took back fruits and 'taters for the master's house. I don't know if the slaves made gifts from their conucos or if the house slaves just took them. A lot of problems with fighting in the barracoons were caused by them. The men arrived and wanted to flirt and fool around with the women.

That's when the worst pushing and shoving began. I was probably twelve years old, and I figured out the whole mess.

There were other tensions, too. For example, between the Congo witch doctor and the Christian there was no getting along. One was good and the other bad. That still goes on in Cuba. The Lucumi and the Congo don't get along either. They bickered over saints and witchcraft. The only ones who didn't have troubles were the old timers from Africa. They were special, and you had to treat them different because they knew all about religion.

Many scuffles were avoided because the masters moved the slaves around. They looked for ways to separate people so there wouldn't be a rash of runaways. That's why the work force never had meetings.

The Lucumís didn't like to work with cane, and many ran away. They were the most rebellious and the bravest. Not the Congos. They were mostly cowards, big on work, so they worked real hard without complaining. There is a well known guinea pig called Conga. She is very cowardly too.

In the plantations there were blacks from different nations. Each one had its own traits. The Congos were dark though you also had many lighter, fair-skinned mulattoes. They were short on the whole. The Mandingos were slightly reddish-colored. Tall and very strong. I swear on my mother's grave they were crooks and a bad bunch. They always went their own way. The Gangas were good folks. Short and freckle faced. Many were cimarrones. The Carabalís were fierce like the Musungo Congos. They didn't kill pigs except on Sundays and the days of Easter. They were very good at business. They ended up killing pigs to sell, and they didn't even eat them. Because of that a song was made for them that went: "Carabalí very needy, kills a pig every Sunday." I got to know all these newly arrived Africans better after slavery ended.

At all the plantations there was an infirmary near the barracoons. It was a large wooden house where they took the pregnant women. Children were born there and stayed until they were six or seven years old when they went to live in the barracoons to work like everyone else. I remember that there were some black nannies who took care of the little slave children and gave them food. When someone was hurt in the field or got sick, those black women would doctor him. With herbs and potions they cured everything. There was no need to worry. Sometimes the little criollitos wouldn't see their parents again because the master was the owner, and he could send them to another plantation. Then the nannies certainly would have to do everything. But who was going to worry about a child that wasn't even her own! In that same infirmary they stripped and bathed the children. The breed stock children cost some 500 pesos. The thing about the breed stock children was that they were born of strong, tall blacks. Tall blacks were privileged. The masters kept an eye out for them to mate them with big healthy black women.

After they were together in a separate room in the barracoon, they were obliged to have sex, and the woman had to bear good babies every year. I tell you it was like breeding animals. Well, if the woman didn't bear the way they liked, they separated them and put her out in the field again to work. The women who weren't like little rabbits were sunk because they had to go back to breaking their backs. Then they could choose a husband at will. There were cases where a woman was after a man, and she herself had twenty women behind her. The witches tried to resolve those matters with powerful magic.

If a man went to a witch to ask for help getting a woman, the witch sent him to get some of the woman's tobacco if she smoked. You ground up the tobacco and a bottle fly, those green, stinging ones, enough to make a powder which you gave to the woman in water. That's how the woman was seduced.

Another treatment was taking the heart of a humming-bird and grinding it into powder. You put it in the woman's tobacco. And if you wanted to make fun of them, all you had to do was send off to the store for barley. Any woman would die of shame on account of that barley because a man would put a little where she was going to sit down, and no sooner than it touched her behind, the woman would begin to break wind. That was a sight to see—those women farting with their faces all powdered up.

The old blacks. entertained themselves with that kind of nonsense. When they were over sixty, they stopped working in the fields. Though, truly, they never knew their real age. But it happened that if a black man got tired and set himself apart, then the overseers said he was ready to be a doorman. Then they put that old man at the gates of the barracoon or at the pig sty, where the big litters were produced. Or, if not that, he helped the women in the kitchen. Some of them had their conucos, and they spent their time gardening. Doing those jobs gave them time for their witchcraft. They weren't punished or paid much attention to. But they had to be quiet and obedient. That's for sure.

I seen many of the horrors of punishment during slavery. That's why I didn't like that life. The cruelest were the stocks that they kept in the boiler house. There were stand-up stocks and lying-down ones. They were made of thick planks with holes where they made the slave put his feet, his hands, and his head. They were locked up like that for two or three months for any kind of simple bad behavior.[5] They used the leather on the pregnant women, too, but they lay them face down over a scooped-out piece of ground to protect their bellies. The women got a whole handful of lashes. Well, they tried not to damage the babies because they wanted them in abundance. The most common type of punishment was whipping. The overseer himself gave out the whippings with a rawhide lash that left marks on the skin. Whips were also made of hemp from any old branch in the woods. It stung like the dickens and tore the skin into little strips. I seen many smart-alecky blacks with their backs red. Afterward they would cover the wounds with compresses of tobacco leaves, urine and salt.

Life was hard, and bodies wore out quick. If you didn't escape early on into the forest to be a cimarrón, you had to be a slave. It was better to be alone, on the loose, than in that corral with all that slime and rot. To make a long story short, life was lonely anyway because women were pretty scarce.[6] And to have a woman you had to be twenty-five years old and lay her in a field. Even the old folks didn't want the young men to have women. They said that twenty-five was when a man ought to have experiences. Many men didn't suffer because they were accustomed to that life. Others had sex with each other and didn't want to have anything to do with women. Sodomy, that was their life. Those men washed clothes, and if they had a husband, they also cooked for him. They were good workers and were busy tending their conucos. They gave the produce to their husbands to sell to the guajiros. And the word effeminate came about after slavery because that situation continued on. In my opinion it didn't come from Africa. Old men didn't like it at all. They wanted to have nothing to do with them. It never mattered to me, sincerely. I believe that everyone marches to his own drummer.

It didn't take much to get tired of living that life. The ones who got used to it didn't have much spirit. Life in the woods was healthier. In the barracoons you caught a lot of diseases. You can say, without exaggeration, that's where a man got sick most often. There were cases of men who had up to three illnesses at the same time. When it wasn't the colic, it was the whooping cough. Colic gave you a pain in the belly that lasted for hours and left you like dead. Whooping cough and the measles were contagious. But the worst, the ones that could cut anybody down, were small pox and the black vomit. Small pox puffed you all up, and the black vomit took you by surprise because it came all of sudden, and between one vomit and another you went stiff. There was a kind of sickness that the whites picked up. It was a sickness of the veins and of a man's private parts. You got rid of it with black women. The man who had it went to bed with a black woman, and it went away. That way they were cured immediately.

In those days there were no powerful medicines. You couldn't find a doctor anywhere. There were the sort of witch nurses who cured you with homemade remedies. Sometimes they cured diseases the doctors didn't understand. Because the problem is not in poking you or pinching your tongue. What you have to do is have confidence in herbs, which are the mother of medicines. The African, from over there, from the other side of the big puddle, he doesn't ever get sick because he has all the herbs within reach.

If some slave caught a contagious disease, they took him out of his room and transferred him to the infirmary. They tried to cure him there. If a slave began to croak, they stuck him in a big box and took him to the cemetery. Usually the overseer came and told the work force to go and bury him. He would say: "Let's go and bury this black man since he has completed his work." And the slaves did it real quick, because, and this is true, when someone died, everybody lowered their heads in mourning.

The cemetery was on the plantation itself, a hundred yards or so from the barracoon. To bury the slaves, they dug a hole in the ground, filled it in, and put up a cross tied together with wire. The cross was to scare off enemies and the devil. Today they say Crucifix. If anyone wears a cross around his neck, it's because someone has thrown some harm at him.

Once they buried a black man, and he got up again. And truth is that he was alive and kicking. They told me that story in Santo Domingo, after slavery. The entire district of Jicotea knows it. The thing happened in a little sugarmill still called El Diamante that belonged to the father of Marinello,[7] the one who talks about Martí a lot. In that place they buried a Congo, and he got up screaming. The people were scared and ran away. A few days later, the Congo man appeared in the barracoon. They say he came in slowly so as not to frighten anyone. But when people saw him they got scared all over again. Then the overseer asked him what had happened, and he said: "They put me in the ground because of cholera, and when I was better, I got out." Since then, every time someone got that disease or any other, they left him for days and days in the box until he was as cold as ice.

These stories are not made up. What I do think is a fiction, because I never seen it ever, is that the blacks committed suicide. Before, when there were Indians in Cuba, suicide did exist. They didn't want to be Christians, and they hung themselves from the trees. But the blacks didn't do that because they went flying, flying in the sky, and headed off for their homeland. The Musundi Congo were the ones who flew the most. They disappeared through witchcraft. They did the same as Canary Island witches but without a sound. There are some who say that the blacks threw themselves into the rivers, but that's a lie. The truth is that they tied a doodad they called a prenda around their waist. That's where the power was. I know that like the palm of my hand, and it's a fact.

The Chinese didn't fly and didn't even want to go back to their homeland. They sure did kill themselves. They did it silently. After several days passed, they appeared hanging from a tree or lying dead on the ground. Everything they did, they did silently. They killed their own overseers with sticks and knives. The Chinese didn't trust anybody. They were rebels from birth. Many times, the master put an overseer of their own race with them to gain their confidence. Him they didn't kill. When slavery was over I met some Chinese in Sagua la Grande, but they were very different and very refined.

Life in the Woods

I have never forgotten the first time I tried to run away. That time I failed and spent a number of years enslaved by the fear they would put the shackles on me again. But I had the spirit of a cimarrón in me, and it didn't go away. I kept quiet about things so nobody could betray me because I was always thinking about escaping. It went round and round in my head and wouldn't leave me in peace. It was an idea that never left me and sometimes even sapped my energy. The old blacks were not kindly towards running away. The women even less so. Runaways, there weren't many. People were afraid of the woods. They said that if some slaves escaped, they would be caught anyway. But for me that idea went around in my head more than any other. I always had the fantasy that I would enjoy being in the forest. And I knew that working in the fields was like living in hell. You couldn't do anything on your own. Everything depended on the master's orders.

One day I began to watch the overseer. I had already been studying him. That dog got stuck in my eyes, and I couldn't get him out. I think he was a Spaniard. I remember that he was tall and never took his hat off. All the blacks had respect for him because one of the whippings he gave could strip the skin off of just about anybody. The thing is, one day I was riled up, and I don't know what got into me, but I was mad, and just seeing him set me off.

I whistled at him from a distance, and he looked around and then turned his back. That's when I picked up a rock and threw it at his head. I know it hit him because he shouted for someone to grab me. But he never saw me again because that day I made it into the woods.

I traveled many days without any clear direction. I was sort of lost. I had never left the plantation. I walked uphill and downhill, all around. I know I got to a farm near Siguanea, where I had no choice but to camp. My feet were full of blisters and my hands were swollen. I camped under a tree. I stayed there no more than four or five days. All I had to do was hear the first human voice close by, and I would take off fast. It would have been real shitty if you got caught right after escaping.

I came to hide in a cave for a time.[8] I lived there for a year and a half. I went in there thinking that I would have to walk less and because the pigs from around the farms, the plots, and the small landholdings used to come to a kind of swamp just outside the mouth of the cave. They went to take a bath and wallow around. I caught them easy enough because big bunches of them came. Every week I had a pig. That cave was very big and dark like the mouth of the wolf. It was called Guajabán. It was near the town of Remedios. It was dangerous because it had no way out. You had to go in through the entrance and leave by the entrance. My curiosity really poked me to find a way out. But I preferred to remain in the mouth of the cave on account of the snakes. The majases are very dangerous beasts. They are found in caves and in the woods. Their breath can't be felt, but they knock people down with it, and then they put people to sleep to suck out their blood. That's why I always stayed alert and lit a fire to scare them away. If you fall asleep in a cave, be ready for the wake. I didn't want to see a majá, not even from a distance. The Congos, and this is true, told me that those snakes lived more than a thousand years. And as they approached two thousand, they became serpents again, and they would return to the ocean to live like any other fish.

Inside, the cave was like a house. A little darker, naturally. Oh, and dung, yes, the smell of bat dung. I walked on it because it was as soft as a mattress. The bats led a life of freedom in the caves. They were and are the masters of them. All over the world it's like that. Since no one kills them, they live a long time. Not as long as the snakes, for sure. The dung they drop works afterward as fertilizer. It becomes dust, and it's thrown on the ground to make pasture for animals and to fertilize crops.

One time that place nearly burned up. I lit a fire, and it spread all through the cave. The bat shit was to blame. After slavery I told the story to a Congo. The story that I had lived with the bats, and that joker, they could sometimes be more jokers than you might imagine, he said: "Listen here, boy, you know nothin'. In my country that thing what you call a bat is big like a pigeon." I knew that was a tall tale. They fooled nearly everyone with those stories. But I heard it, and smiled inside.

The cave was quiet. The only sound always there was the bats going: "Chwee, chwee, chwee." They didn't know how to sing. But they talked to each other and understood each other. I saw that one would say "Chewy, chewy, chewy," and the bunch would go wherever he went. They were very united about things. Bats have no wings. They're nothing but a cloth with a little black head, very dirty, and if you get up real close, you'll see they look like rats. In the cave I was summering, you might say. What I really liked was the woods, and after a year and a half I left that darkness behind. I took to the footpaths. I went into the woods in Siguanea again. I spent a long time there. I took care of myself like a spoiled child. I didn't want to be chained to slavery again.

For me that was disgusting. I've always thought so. Slavery was a nuisance. I still think so today.

I was careful about all the sounds I made. And of the fires. If I left a track, they could follow my path and catch me. I climbed up and down so many hills that my legs and arms got as hard as sticks. Little by little I got to know the woods. And I was getting to like them. Sometimes I would forget I was a cimarrón, and I would start to whistle. Early on I used to whistle to get over the fear. They say that when you whistle, you chase away the evil spirits. But being a cimarrón in the woods you had to be on the lookout. I didn't start whistling again because the guajiros or the slave catchers could come. Since the cimarrón was a slave who had escaped, the masters sent a posse of rancheadores after them. Mean guajiros with hunting dogs so they could drag you out of the woods in their jaws. I never ran into any of them. I never seen one of those dogs up close. They were trained to catch blacks. If a dog saw a black man, he ran after him. If by chance I heard one barking nearby, I took my clothes right off because the dog can't smell anybody naked like that. When I see a dog now, nothing happens, but if I seen one then, all of me you would see would be my heels. I've never been attracted to dogs. To my mind they have wicked instincts.

When a slave catcher caught a black, the master or the overseer gave him an ounce of gold or more. In those years, an ounce was like saying seventeen pesos. Who knows how many guajiros were in that business!

Truth is that I lived well as a cimarrón, very hidden, very comfortable. I didn't even allow other cimarrones to spot me: "cimarrón with cimarrón sells a cimarrón."

I didn't do many other things. For a long time I didn't speak a word to anyone. I liked that tranquility. Other cimarrones always went around in groups of two or three. But that was dangerous because when it rained, their footprints stayed in the mud. That's how they caught many foolish groups.

There was a kind of black who was a freeman. I used to see them in the woods searching for herbs and guinea pigs, but I never called to them or approached them. Just the opposite, when I saw one of those blacks what I did was hide more carefully. Some worked in the crop lands, and when they left the field, I took the opportunity to go in and carry off the 'taters and pigs. They almost always had pigs on their conucos. But I would rather rob things from the small land holdings because they had more of everything. And it was easier. The small land holdings were bigger than the conucos. Much bigger! They were more like farms. The blacks didn't have those luxuries. The guajiros sure did live easy, in houses of thatch, cane thatch or real palm. From the distance I could see them playing music. Sometimes I could even hear them. They played little accordions, guitars, bandor guitars, kettledrums, calabash, maracas, and hollow gourds. Those were their main instruments. When I left the woods was when I came to learn their names because as a cimarrón I was ignorant of everything.

They liked to dance. But they didn't dance to the music of the blacks. They tended toward the zapateo and the caringa. All the guajiros got together in the afternoon, around five to dance the zapateo. The men put a kerchief around their necks, and the women put them on their heads. If a guajiro really danced well, his woman would come to put a hat on top of the one he had on. It was the prize. I came up to them carefully, and I was able to take it all in. I even seen the pianolas. They played all the instruments there. They made a lot of noise, but it was real pretty. From time to time a guajiro grabbed for a gourd to accompany the pianola. It was on those instruments that you could hear the popular music of the times, the danzón.

On Sundays the guajiros dressed all in white. The women wore their hair down and put flowers in it. Then they went to the partidos, and they got together there in the taverns made out of wood to have parties. The men like to wear canvas and heavy drill cloth. They made long shirts that resembled guayaberas with open pockets. Guajiros in those years lived better than people imagine. Almost everyday they got a bonus from the masters. They were friendly with each other and did their dirty work together. I think that the cimarrón lived better than the guajiro. The cimarrón was more free.

To look for food you had to be carrying things back and forth, but there was always enough food. "The cautious tortoise carries its house on its back." What I liked most were 'taters and pig meat. I think it was because of pig meat that I've lasted so long. I ate it every day, and it never did me any harm. To catch little pigs I went up to the small farms at night, making sure no one heard me. The first one I saw I grabbed by the neck, and swung him up on my shoulder with a rope tight around him and took off running, with a hand over his snout. When I found a place to camp, I lay him down on one side, and I began to look him over. If he was fed well and weighed about twenty pounds, then I had food for sure for fifteen days.

You live half wild when you're a cimarrón. I myself hunted animals like the guinea pigs. The guinea pig is fast as the devil, and to catch it you have to have lightning in your feet. I liked smoked guinea pig a great deal. Nowadays, I don't know what people think of that animal, but no one eats it. I used to catch a guinea pig and smoke it without salt and it would last me for months. The guinea pig is the healthiest food there is, although 'taters are the best thing for your bones. If you eat them everyday, especially taro, you won't have bone trouble. In the woods there are lots of those wild 'taters. The taro has a big leaf that shines at night. You recognize it right away.

All the leaves in the woods have uses. Tobacco or mulberry leaves work for bites. Whenever I saw that the bite of some bug was going to get swollen up on me, I took hold of the tobacco leaf, and I chewed it well. Then I put it on the bite, and the swelling went down. Often when it was cold, an ache seeped into my bones. It was a dry pain that didn't go away. To rid myself of it I made a brew of rosemary leaves, and it went away right then. The cold also gave me a bad cough. The sniffles and a cough was what I got. That was when I picked a big leaf and put it on my chest. I never found out the name of that leaf, but it gave off a whitish liquid that was very warm. That soothed my cough. When I got very cold my eyes would water up, and they itched in a very bothersome way. The same thing happened to me with the sun. In that case I would put out a few leaves of the ítamo plant to catch the dew, and the next day clean my eyes with them. Itamo is the best thing there is for that. Nowadays what they sell in the pharmacy is ítamo. What happens is that they put it in little jars, and it seems like something else. As one gets old, the thing with your eyes goes away. I haven't suffered from itching for many years.

I smoked the leaf of the macaw tree. I made well-rolled, tightly-packed cigars with it. After I left the woods, I didn't smoke tobacco any more, but while I was a cimarrón, I smoked it all the time.

And I drank coffee. I made coffee with guanina leaf. I had to grind the leaf with a bottle. After it was well broken up, I boiled it, and then it was coffee. You could always put a little wild honey in it to give it flavor. With the honey the coffee gave strength to the body. You're always fortified when you live in the woods.

Being weak comes from town life because people go crazy over lard when they see it. I never liked it because it makes you weak. If you eat a lot of lard, you get fat and sort of dumb. Lard does bad things to the circulation and strangles people. One of the best remedies to keep your health is bee honey. You can get it easy in the woods. Anywhere you wanted there was bee honey. I found loads of it in the hollows of trees. Honey was used to make canchánchara which was a delicious water drink. It was made with river water and honey. The best thing was to drink it cold. That water was better for you than any of today's medicine. It was natural. When there was no river nearby, I used to go deep into the woods to look for a spring. In the woods there are enough springs to make sweet water. They ran downhill and brought the coldest, clearest water I ever seen in my life.

The simple truth is that I never needed anything in the woods. The only thing I couldn't have was sex. Since there were no women, I had to get by with my desire bottled up. You couldn't even step up to a mare because they neighed like the dickens. And when the guajiros heard that clamor they would come right away, and nobody was going to put cuffs on me just for a mare.

I never went without fire. The first days I spent in the woods I carried matches. Then they ran out, and I had to use tinder. It was a black ash that I kept in a tinderbox the Spaniards sold in the taverns. It was very easy to make a fire.

All you had to do was strike the tinderbox with a stone till it made a spark. I learned that from the Canary Islanders when I was a slave. I never liked the Islanders. They were very bossy and very stingy. The Galicians were better people and got along better with the blacks.

Since I've always liked to be my own boss, I kept myself away from them. From everyone. I even stayed away from the animals. So the snakes wouldn't come up close, I lit a thick log and left it to burn all night long. The snakes didn't approach because they thought the fire was the devil or one of their enemies. That's why I say I felt good being a cimarrón. Because I was my own boss, and I defended myself on my own. I used knives and short Collin machetes which were the ones the rural police used. Those weapons were used to cut down the forest or to hunt animals. And I had them ready in case some slave catchers wanted to catch me by surprise. Though that would have been hard because I kept on the move. I walked so much in the sun that my head would begin to get hot and sort of red, for me. Then I would get some hot spells that were so fierce that to get over them I had to wrap up some, almost always with a plantain leaf, or put fresh herbs on my forehead. The trouble was that I had no hat, which is why my head would get all heated up that way. I used to figure that the heat got into my insides and softened up my brains.

Once the hot spell passed (sometimes it lasted for many days), I would slip into the first river I saw without making a sound and come out like new. River water did me no harm. I think river water is the best thing for your health because it's cold. That cold is good because it makes you hard. Your bones feel in place. Rain water gave me some sniffles, which I got rid of with a brew of cuajaní berries and bee honey. To stay dry I covered myself with yagua palm fronds. I folded them over a stand I made with four forked stakes, and I fashioned a shelter. Those shelters were seen all around after slavery and during the war. They looked like lean-tos.

What I did most was walk and sleep. When it got to be midday or five in the afternoon, I used to hear the conch shell that the women would use to call their husbands. It sounded like: "foooo, foo, foo, foo, foo." At night I slept like a log. That's why I was so fat. I didn't think about a thing. It was only eat and sleep and watch. I used to like to go to the hillsides at night. The hills were quieter and safer. Slave catchers or wild animals were unlikely to go there. I almost reached Trinidad. From up on those hills you could see the town. And the ocean.

The closer I got to the coast, the bigger the ocean became. I always figured it was a giant river. At times I stared at it, and it became the strangest white and got lost in my eyes. The ocean is another big mystery of nature. And it's very important because it can carry men off, swallow them, and never give them back. Those are what are called shipwrecked people.

What I do remember well are the birds in the woods. I haven't forgotten that. I remember them all. There were pretty ones and some right ugly ones. At first, they put a lot of fear into me, but later I became accustomed to hearing them. I really believed they were watching out for me. The cotunto was the most bothersome one. It was a black bird, pitch black, that sang: "You, you, you, you, you ate the cheese I had over there." And it repeated that until I answered, "Get out of here!" and it flew away. I used to hear him crystal clear. There was another one that answered him like a ghost, going "coo, coo, coo, coo, coo, coo."

The gnome owl was one of the ones that scared you the most. It always came at night. The ugliest thing in the woods was that critter! It had white feet and yellow eyes. It screamed something like this: "cous, cous, couououous."

The barn owl sang a sad song, but it was a witch. It searched for dead mice. It sang: "chew-ah, chew-ah, chew-ah, kuwee, kuwee," and it flew off like lightning. When I saw an owl in my path, especially when she went back and forth, I wouldn't go on because by doing that she was giving warning that there was an enemy or death itself nearby. The owl is wise and strange. I remember that the male witches had a lot of respect for her and did magic with the barn owl or sunsundamba, which is what she is called in Africa. The owl has probably left Cuba. I haven't seen her again. Those birds change their territory.

The house sparrow came from Spain and has produced quite a number of offspring here.

And the tocoloro which is more or less green. The tocoloro has a scarlet band across his chest that's the same as the sash the King of Spain wears. The overseers said he was the King's messenger. What I know is that you couldn't even look at the tocoloro. The black man who killed one of those birds was killing the King. I seen many blacks get the lash for killing tocoloros and sparrows. I liked that bird because it sang as though it was hopping around, going, "coh, co, coh, co, coh, co."

The one that sure was a mother's whore was the ciguapa owl. It whistled just like a man. Anybody would get a chill hearing it. I don't want to think about how many times those creatures bothered me.

In the forest I got used to living with the trees. They also have their sounds because the leaves whistle in the wind. There is a tree with a big white leaf. At night it seems like a bird. In my opinion, that tree spoke. It made "ooch, ooch, we, we, ooch, ooch." Trees have shadows too. The shadows don't do harm, though at night you shouldn't walk on them. I think the shadows of trees are like a man's spirit. The spirit is the reflection of the soul. You can see that. What men are surely not able to see is the soul. We can't say that the soul has such and such a color. The soul is one of the greatest things in the world. Dreams are made for making contact with it. The old Congos said that the soul was like witchcraft one had on the inside. They also said that there were good spirits and evil spirits, that is, good souls and bad souls. And that everybody had them. In my opinion, there are some who have a soul for witchcraft and nothing more. Other people have natural ones. I prefer the natural one because the other means a pact with the devil. And the soul can leave the body. That happens when a person dies or when he sleeps. That is, when the soul leaves on its own and begins to move around. It does that to rest because so much struggle all the time would be unbearable

There are people who don't like to be called when they're sleeping because they frighten easily, and they can die all of a sudden. That happens because during sleep the soul leaves the body. It leaves a person empty. I sometimes have the shakes at night. It was the same in the woods. So I cover myself good because that's the warning God sends you so you'll take care of yourself. If you suffer from the shakes, you have to pray a lot.

The heart is very different. It never leaves its place. Just by putting your hand on the left side you can prove that it's beating. But the day it stops, you have to be ready to go. That's why you shouldn't trust it.

Now, the most important thing about this subject is the angel. The Guardian Angel. He's the one who makes you go forward or go backward. For me the angel ranks higher than the soul and the heart, always at the foundation of a person, caring for him, watching everything. It will not leave for anything in the world. I've thought a lot about these things, and I still see them a little in the dark. All these thoughts come while one is alone. A man thinks at all hours. Even when he's dreaming it's as though he was thinking. It's not good to speak about those thoughts. There is the danger that decay will set in. You can't trust people very much. How many people ask you questions to find out about you, and then split your hide down the middle! Besides, the question about spirits is infinite, like numbers that never come to an end. No one knows where they end.

Truth is that I don't even trust the Holy Ghost. That's why as a cimarrón I remained alone. I did nothing but listen to the birds and the trees, and eat, but I never met anyone. I remember I was so hairy that my kinka got all tangled up together That was scary. When I went into town, a old man called Tá Migué cut my hair with a big scissors. He gave me a trim that made me like a fancy horse. I felt strange with all that wool off. I was awful cold. Within a few days my hair began to grow again. Blacks have that tendency. I never seen a bald black man. Not one. The Spaniards brought baldness to Cuba.

All my life I've liked the woods. But when slavery ended I stopped being a cimarrón. I found out about the end of slavery from all the people shouting, and I left the woods. They shouted, "We're free now." But I wasn't affected. To my mind, it was a lie. I don't know...fact was that I went up to a mill, and without touching the boilers or the cans or anything, I stuck my head out little by little until I came out altogether in the open. That was when Martínez Campos[9] was governor because the slaves said he was the one who let them go free. Even so, many years passed in Cuba, and there were still slaves. It lasted longer than people believe.

When I came out of the woods I started in walking, and I met an old woman with two children in her arms. I called to her from a distance, and when she came up to me I asked her: "Tell me, is it true that we're no longer slaves?" She answered me: "No, son, now we're really free." I kept walking the way I was headed, and I started to look for work. Many blacks wanted to be friends of mine. And they asked me what I did as a cimarrón. And I told them: "Nothing." I've always liked independence. Sassy talk and idle gossip do no good. I went for years and years without talking to anyone.

THE ABOLITION OF SLAVERY

Life in the Sugarmills

After all that time I was in the woods I was really sort of wild I didn't want to work anywhere. I was afraid they were going to lock me in. I well knew that slavery hadn't ended completely. People would ask me what I was doing, and they wanted to know where I was from. Sometimes I told them: "I am Esteban. I was a cimarrón." Other times I said I had worked in such and such a sugarmill and that I wasn't able to find my relatives. I must have been about twenty years old already. Even then I hadn't located my relatives. That came later.

Since I didn't know anybody, for a long time I went from town to town. I didn't starve because people gave me food. Just saying you had no work always made someone toss you a little something. But you can't go on like that. And I realized that I had to work in order to eat and sleep, in a barracoon at least. I had already been around quite a bit when I decided that I would cut cane. I knew that whole area in the northern part of Las Villas pretty well. That's the prettiest part of Cuba. I started working around there.

The first mill I worked at was called Purio. I arrived one day in the rags I was wearing and a hat I had picked up. I went in and asked the overseer if he had work. He told me he did. I recall he was a Spaniard, with moustaches, by the name of Pepe. There were overseers in these parts until a short time ago. The difference being that they didn't hit you like during slavery. They were of the same breed though, big mouthed, bitter men. There were still barracoons in those mills after Abolition. They were the same as before. Many were like new because they were made of cement. Others had fallen down from rain and storms. At Purio, the barracoon was sturdy and looked as if it had just been built. They told me to go and live there. When I got there, I settled in right away. The place wasn't so bad. They took the locks off the barracoons, and the workers themselves had made holes in the walls for ventilation. There was no more worry that somebody would escape or any of that. Blacks were already free. What was called freedom because I realized that horrible things still went on. And there were masters, or rather, owners, who believed that blacks were made for locking up and whipping. So they treated them the same as before. To my mind many blacks didn't realize things had changed because they kept on saying: "Your blessing, Master."

They wouldn't leave the mill for anything at all. I was different in that I didn't even deal with the white man. They believed they were the owners of humanity. At Purio I always lived alone. From Easter to the feast of San Juan I could keep a mistress. But women have always been money hungry, and in those times there was no man alive who could maintain a black woman. Even though I do claim that women are the most important thing in the world. I never was lacking for a woman who said to me "I want to live with you."

The first months on the sugarmill I felt strange. I felt strange like that for some three months. I got tired out from nothing at all. My hands peeled and my feet kept swelling up on me. It seems to me it was the cane that made me like that, the cane and the sun. Since I was worn out like that, I stayed in the barracoon at night to rest. Until I got accustomed to it. Sometimes I thought of going out at night.

Fact is that there were dances in the towns and other entertainments, but I didn't want to do anything but look for women to play around with.

The work was exhausting. You spent hours in the field, and it seemed that that work would never end. It went on and on until it left you wrung out. The overseers constantly pushing. The worker who rested for long was taken off the job. I worked from six in the morning. That hour didn't bother me because in the woods you can't sleep until late anyway on account of the roosters. At eleven in the morning they gave you a break for lunch. Lunch had to be eaten in the eating house in the batey—almost always standing up because of the number of people crowding the place. At one o'clock in the afternoon you went back to the fields. That's the worst time and the hottest hour. Work ended at six in the evening. Then I would up and go to the river. I took a bath for a while and then went to get something to eat. I had to hurry because the kitchen didn't serve at night.

Food cost about six pesos a month. They gave a good-sized portion though it was always the same—rice and black beans, white beans or black eyed peas and beef jerky. Once in a while they killed an old ox. Beef is good, but I prefer pork. It fills you up more and gives you strength. 'Taters were the best of all, sweet potato, taro, yam. Flour, too, but if you have to eat it all by itself everyday, it gets tiresome. Flour wasn't in short supply there. Some workers were in the habit of going to the overseer's office for authorization to get the uncooked food and take it to the barracoon. They cooked on their own fires. A man who had a steady woman ate with her. That's what I did, too, because when I had a steady woman, I wasn't going to suffer through the heat and suffocation of the eating house.

The blacks who worked at Purio had almost all of them been slaves. And they were used to the life of a barracoon; that's why they didn't go out to eat. When lunchtime came, they went into their rooms with their women and ate lunch. The same at dinner time. They didn't go out at night. They were afraid of people and said they were going to get lost. They were convinced of that. I couldn't think like that because if I got lost, I was able to find my bearings. I don't know many times I found my way in the woods without ever locating a river!

Sundays all the workers who wanted to could work the faina.[10] That meant that instead of resting you went to the fields, cleared with a machete, stripped or cut cane. Or if not that, you stayed at the mill cleaning the troughs or scraping the boilers. This would only be in the morning. Since there was nothing special to be done on that day, the workers always used to go to earn extra money. Money is a very bad thing. A person who gets used to earning a lot of money is ruined. I earned what everybody else did. The pay came out be some twenty-four pesos, including the food. Some mills paid twenty-five pesos.

There were still a lot of taverns nearby where you could spend money. At Purio there were two or three. I used to go regularly to buy a drink or whatever else I needed. Fact is, the taverns weren't very good places. Almost every day there were fights over women out of envy or jealousy. At night they had fiestas. Everybody who wanted to could go to those fiestas. They were in the bateyes. There was space to dance, and the blacks themselves sang the rumbas. The guasabeo was a milling around drunken bash. I never got mixed up in that, I mean, not completely. I watched it all when I felt like it. If not, I stayed behind to rest. Time would go flying by.

At nine on the dot, the rumba drums had to be put away because the silence bell, the loudest one there was, was rung then for bed time. If it had been up to the blacks, they would have stayed up dancing till dawn. I really know how it was for them. You can still go to a dance, and the last to leave will be a black for sure. As for myself, I can't say I don't like dancing and the rumba, but it so happens that I'm given to taking the long view. In the morning folks would get up already worn out. But they kept right on as if there was no tomorrow.

In the mills at that time you could work steady or part-time. The ones who worked full-time had the obligation to work fixed hours. They made a contract for several months. By doing that, they could live in the barracoon and needn't leave the mill for anything at all. I liked working steady because the other way life was very busy. The ones who decided to work on their own just went to the cane field and made a deal. They could take a lot two or three besanas long and make arrangements depending on the quantity of weeds. In those years that could be arranged for thirty or forty pesos. And the work of clearing them could be done in fifteen or sixteen days. Those workers were smart. They could take a break every little bit, go get a drink of water, and they even kept their women in the weeds to have sex with them there. After the days passed and the land was good and clean, the mayordomo came to inspect it. If he found some shoots, they had to go over it again. The mayordomo came back, and if he was satisfied, they went off with their money to roam around the towns until the weeds began to grow again. If their money ran out quick, they looked for a way to go to another mill to work. They were always drifters. They lived in the barracoons, too, but in smaller rooms. They almost never took their women to their rooms. They saw them at night because they did have permission to go out after their faina.

It was different with those of us who worked steady. We couldn't go out at night because at nine we had to be ready for the silence bell. Sundays were the days I went out in the afternoon and stayed late. There were nights when I arrived after nine. And nothing happened to me. They opened up for me and told me: "Get a move on, you're late, you bastard!"

The barracoons were a little humid, but even so they were safer than the woods. There were no snakes. All us workers slept in hammocks. They were comfortable, and you could cover up good when it was cold. Many of the barracoons were made out of sacks. The only bothersome thing about the barracoons were the fleas. They did no harm, but you had to keep scaring them away all night with feverfew. It gets rid of fleas and ticks. All you had to do was spread a little on the floor. If you ask me, all those bugs were born in Cuba as the Indians' revenge. Cuban territory is hexed by them. They are getting even for their dead. Hatuey and all his tribe.

At Purio, like in all the other mills, there were slaves from several countries in Africa. But the Congos were the biggest group. They didn't call that whole northern region of Las Villas Congo land for nothing. In those days there also were the Filipinos, the Chinese, Canary Islanders, and there were more and more criollos. They all worked cane, spaded, cleared weeds with machetes, hilled over the dirt. To hill over is to plow with a lead boy and an ox to turn the earth, just like during slavery.

Relations between the groups remained the same. The Filipinos carried on with their criminal instincts. The Canary Islanders didn't talk. For them work was everything. They were still dolts. Since I didn't make friends with them, they got mad at me. You have be careful with the Islanders because they know a lot about witchcraft. They can do a bad turn to just about anybody. I think they earned more than the blacks, though it was said back then that everyone earned the same. The mayordomo of the mill took care of the pay. He kept all the accounts. He was usually a Spaniard, too, and an old man. The mayordomos were old because you have to have a lot of experience to do the accounts. He paid all the workers at the mill. After the owner checked the books, the mayordomo announced we could get paid. We were called in by name. One by one we went inside the office or into the storeroom, depending. There were some who preferred to take all their money in cash. Others, like me, preferred for the mayordomo himself to give a chit for food to the storekeeper so we could buy on the tab. The storekeeper was the one who gave us the money. Half for food and drinks, and the other in cash. It was better that way because you didn't have to go into that office so they could look you up and down. I've always preferred independence. Besides, the storekeepers were nice, retirees from the Spanish army.

In those days they paid in Mexican or Spanish money. Mexican coins were silver, big and shiny, called carandolesas. There were smaller coins of twenty cents, forty cents or one peso. I remember a Spanish one called Amadeo I. A person who got one of those in his hands didn't spend it. He saved it like a keepsake because Amadeo I was King of Spain. They were made of pure silver like the Isabelinas, which were worth fifty cents. Almost all the rest were made of gold. There were two peso escudos, doubloons that were worth four pesos, gold centenes, with a value of five pesos thirty cents, one ounce and half ounce coins.

Those were the coins that circulated the most in Cuba until the coronation of Alfonso XIII. I learned them by heart so I didn't get cheated. It was easier then than now because they all had the head of a king or a queen or a coat of arms on them. King Alfonso XIII had pesetas and silver pesos sent here. The calderilla was made of copper, and they were worth a cent and two cents. Others came like the real fuerte which was worth fifteen cents. If you count right, twenty reales fuertes makes three pesos. That's true no matter how you add it up. There are still folks who cling to the old ways of counting with those coins. It seems they think that mankind makes no progress. Although you might like old habits, you can't spend you life repeating them like a squeaky wheel.

I was better off then than now. I had my youth. Now I can have my steady woman once in a while, but it's not the same. A woman is a great thing. The truth is that what I've most enjoyed in my life have been the women. Back then, when I was there at Purio, I up and went to town on Sundays, always in the afternoon, so as to not lose out on the morning faina. And sometimes even before getting to town I got me a woman. I was very bold. I struck up a conversation with any old pretty dark woman, and they would let themselves fall for me. I always told them the truth, that's for sure. I told them I was a laborer and that I liked to be sincere. You couldn't go around being cute with women like nowadays. No sir! Women in those days were worth as much as the men. They worked as much, and they had no appreciation at all for those useless drifters. If I got a woman to trust me, I could even ask her for money. Now, she would try to see if I needed it or not. And if I did, she would give me all I asked for. If not, she sent me packing. Those were women in the old days.

When a man found himself short on women, he went to the Sunday fiestas in the town closest to the mill. There were dances in the streets and in the social clubs. The streets filled up with folks dancing and having a grand old time. I went for no other reason than to get women because I've never liked dancing. People played cards and raced horses. They used to put up two poles at one end of the street and tie a rope across from one side to the other. From the rope they hung a ring, and the rider had to run a stick or puá, as they called it, through the ring. If he did, he won a prize. Usually the prize was to strut around town on the horse. And be the proudest one there. That's why so many riders came from other nearby towns. I used to like to stand in the fields where the races were and watch the horses. What I didn't like was the way people began quarreling and picking fights. It didn't take much to stir up bad feelings at the races. Blacks paid no mind to any of that. They saw it and all, but...What black man had a good horse?

The best entertainment was the cock fight. It was held on Sundays in every town. In Calabazar de Sagua, which was the closest to Purio, there was a large cock pit. The pits were all made of wood and painted red and white. The roof was made out of boards with a big piece of cardboard to cover the cracks. The fights were bloody. But there wasn't a man in those days who didn't go to see them. The blood was an attraction and a diversion, strange as it may seem. It worked to get money away from the cane sugar farmers who were beginning to get rich back then. The laborers also bet. Cock fights were a vice. They still are. Once you got inside the pit you just had to keep on gambling. That's no place for cowards. Or bums. During the fights anyone could go wild. The shouting was worse than the blood. You couldn't stand the heat. Even so, men went to try their luck. Both whites and blacks would go to gamble. The problem was having the gold coins to bet. What black man had any! Aside from the cock fights and getting drunk, there was nothing much to do. It was better to go with a woman to the woods and lie down together.

When the feast of San Juan came, which is the 24th of June, there were fiestas in many towns. Everything was all spruced up for that day. They celebrated it at Calabazar, and I went over to see. There wasn't a man or woman who didn't wear their best clothes to go to town. Material in those days was different from today. In general, men wore canvas shirts or striped ones. Those striped shirts were very elegant, and they fastened with gold buttons. They also wore Jipijapa cloth; almud, which was a cloth as black as tar; and very shiney alpaca. It was said to be the most expensive. I never wore it. A coarse woolen cloth of a gray color was quite common. The best pants were made with it. I wore that a lot because it hid the dirt.

In those days, men liked to dress well. Myself, if I had no clothes, I didn't go to town. And then there's that business about the cimarrón being known as a savage. At least that's what ordinary people said. If you compare clothes back then to today, there's no way to explain why people didn't bake in the hot season.

Women's clothes were the limit. The women looked like walking wardrobes. I think they draped themselves with everything they could find. They wore a slip, a skirt, petticoats, a corset, and on top a wide dress with colored ribbons and bows. Their wardrobe was almost all fine linen. They also wore bustles. A bustle was like a small pillow the width of the buttocks. They attached it to their waist and let it fall down behind so their buttocks would shake. To have a bustle was like having false flesh. Some padded their bust. I don't know how they fixed it up, but it looked real. I knew it was rags and all, but to see a woman like that, all jutting out, sure was something. The ones without much hair wore hairpieces. Hair styles were prettier then than today. And natural. They did their own hair, and they always left it long because that was the Spanish fashion. From Spain, because none of the fashions came from Africa. I didn't like the women who cut their hair short. They looked like boys. The matter of short hair came up when hairdressers started up in Cuba. Before that, it was unheard of. Women were the main attraction at the fiestas. They pretended to be more religious than anybody. That's where all that covering up came from. Everything they wore was good quality. And they made sure everybody knew it. Gold earrings and bracelets, shoes of all kinds, of kid, and boots with heels that had a little metal tip to protect the toe. The shoes had button fasteners. There was a kind of boot called a Polish boot that buttoned only on the side. Men wore high boots with elastic at the ankle. But they were for men with money. I, for example, had nothing but a pair of low cut, leather shoes and my cowhide slippers.

The fiestas of San Juan were the best known in that area. Two or three days before the 24th the children of the town began to make the preparations. They decorated the houses and the church with palm fronds. The adults organized the dances in the clubs. At that time there were already black societies, with a cantina and a dance floor. They charged an entrance fee that went to the society's funds. Sometimes I went up to those places, took off my straw hat, and went in. But I left right away on account of the crowds. Men used to the outdoors weren't in the habit of dancing in such close quarters. Besides, the women would come outside and that was where you could catch them. When I saw a woman leave, I went up to her and asked her to have a drink or something to eat. There were always stands selling popovers, little meat pies, sausages, tamales, cider, and beer. Now they call these stands kiosks. The beer they sold was Spanish, brand T. It cost twenty-five centavos, and was ten times stronger than modern beer. A beer drinker liked its bitter taste. I had me a few and felt good and high.

The cider was good too, and people drank a lot of it. Above all at baptisms. They say that cider is sacred, gold water.

Rioja wine was very popular. I knew about it from the time of slavery. It came to be about twenty-five reales a pitcher, or two pesos and fifty cents. A glass cost half a peso or a real, depending on the size. That wine made all the women tipsy. You should see one of those mamas tipsy, wobbling off into the woods...

Although that fiesta was a religious affair because they even had altars in the doorways to houses, I never managed to pray. Never seen other men praying either. They went to drink and pick up women. The streets were full of vendors selling corn fritters, sweet popovers, grapefruits, coconuts, and natural juices.

It was the custom in those fiestas to dance the caringa. The caringa was a white man's dance. They danced in pairs with kerchiefs in their hands. They formed groups to dance it in the park or on the streets. It seemed like they were Carnival groups. They jumped quite a bit. They played accordions, gourds, and kettle drums. And they sang:

> Swing and swing and swing caringa
> give my old lady a slap and zingah

Swing and swing and swing caringa
give my old lady a slap and zingah

They also danced the zapateo, which is the original
Cuban dance, and the tumbandera. The zapateo was very
showy. That dance wasn't as indecent as the African ones.
The dancers didn't touch or even come close with their
bodies. It was danced in family houses or out in the country.
It didn't have to be a special day. You could dance the
zapateo on the 24th of June as well as on the Day of San
Diego. To dance the zapateo, the women wore very elegant
Dutch linen, and they put little bunches of flowers in their
hair, fancy flowers, not any of those wild flowers. They
decorated their dresses with embroidered ribbons and wore
red and white scarves. The men also put on kerchiefs and
straw hats. The women stood in front of the men and began
to stomp their heels while holding their skirts up. And the
men looked at them and laughed. And they circled around
them with their hands behind their backs. Sometimes a
woman picked up her partner's hat from the ground and
put it on. They did that for fun. Many of the men who saw
that threw their hats down, and their partners would go
picking them up to put them on. Women dancers were
given presents, of money and flowers. Before, flowers were
more appreciated. There were flowers everywhere. You
never see flowers nowadays like you did then on fiesta days. I
remember that all the houses were decorated with flowers.
They tied small bunches of flowers on a little wire they hung
from the railings above the doorways. The families
themselves threw flowers into the street to anyone who
passed by. There used to be a rose, a big rose, called the
Bourbon Rose. That flower and the lily were the ones that
sold the most. The lily is white and has a strong scent.

Carnations and roses, the best flowers in the Spanish Colonia. That's where they danced the jota. The jota was exclusively for the Spanish. They brought that dance to Cuba, and they didn't let anyone else dance it. To see it, I stood in the big gateway of the Colonia and looked inside. Fact is that the jota was pretty because of the costumes they wore to dance it. And because of the castanets. They raised their arms and laughed like a bunch of idiots. They went on like that all night long. Sometimes those same Spaniards saw that people were crowded together in the windows watching, and so they came out and gave you wine, grapes, and cheese. I drank a good deal of Spanish wine by using the tactic of standing in the gateway.

The tumbandera was another popular dance. It has also disappeared. The whites didn't dance it because they said it was the black mob's dance. I didn't like it, to tell the truth. The jota was more refined. The tumbandera resembled the rumba. Very lively. A man and a woman always danced it together. They played two little drums similar to the tumbadoras. But they were much smaller. And the maracas. You could dance it in the street or in the Societies of Color.

The fiestas today are not the great success of the old days. They are more modern or who knows what...The fact is that you had a real good time in those years. Myself, I would go just to watch, and I had a good time. People wore different costumes of loud colors. They wore cloth and cardboard masks to look like devils or monkeys or clowns. If a man wanted to take revenge on another, for whatever reason, he dressed up like a woman, and when he saw his enemy pass by, he would give him a crack with his whip and take off running. That way no one could catch him.

Various games were organized for the fiestas of San Juan. The one I remember most was the game of the ducks. It was a bit cruel because you had to kill a duck. After the duck was good and dead, they took it by its feet and covered it with lard. The duck glistened. Then they hung it from a rope stretched between two poles stuck in the ground on either side of the street. More people went to see this game than to the dance. After they had the duck strung up on that rope, the riders came out. They started out at a distance of ten meters. And they began to gallop. They had to pick up speed or it didn't count, and when they got to the duck, they had to yank its head off with all their might. The one who managed to take it off was awarded a scarlet sash and was named the President of the Dance. As President he received other favors. Women immediately crowded around him. If he had a girlfriend, they put another sash on her and named her the First Lady. That night they both presided at the dance. They were the first to take the dance floor. Flowers were tossed at them, too.

In the morning, around ten, they lit the Judas. The Judas was a stick doll very similar to a man. They strung a rope through him over the middle of the street. That doll represented the devil himself. Boys set him on fire, and since he was covered with paper, he went up immediately. You could see those colored papers burning in the air, and the head, and the arms...I seen that for many years because that custom continued for a long time. The Day of San Juan everybody went to swim in the river. Those who didn't swim got covered with bugs real quick. If there was someone who couldn't go down to the river, like an old lady or a very small child, they got into a tub. A washtub wasn't the same as a river, but it had water in it, and that was the idea. The more water you poured on yourself, the more bugs you got off. A black woman was my mistress, and she was like a cat about water. Even so, on San Juan's day she got in the river with all her clothes on.

Since the santeros gave their fiestas on that day too, I took a little time at night and went over there. I stopped in at several places, greeted folks and the saints, and went home to rest. There was a custom that the godchildren took gold coins to their godparents. And whatever other thing they might ask for. For blacks a godfather and godmother were the greatest thing there ever was because they were the ones who gave you your saint. The fiestas in the Casas de Santería were very good. Only black people went there. The Spaniards didn't approve of that. As the years went by things changed. Today you can see a white babalao priest with red cheeks. But it was different then because santería is an African religion. Not even the Civil Guards, the pure blooded ones would have anything to do with it. They passed by and at most asked a question: "What's going on?" And the blacks answered: "Here we are, celebrating San Juan." They said San Juan, but it was Oggún. Oggún is the god of war. In those years he was the best known in the area. He's always found in the countryside, and they dress him in green or purple. Oggún Arere, Oggún Oké, Oggún Aguanillé.

You had to be very respectful when you went to the saint's fiesta. If you didn't believe, you had to hide it. Blacks don't like intruders. They have never liked them. That's why I went real quiet. I listened to the drums. I watched the blacks, and I ate something. I always ate something at a saint's fiesta. And there was always food left over. All kinds. What I liked most was amalá flour. That was Changó's food. It was made with corn meal and water. When the corn was boiling, they peeled it, and they took off its husks. They threw it in a pestle, and ground and ground until it was mush.

Then the amalá was wrapped in a banana leaves in little balls. It could be eaten with sugar or plain.

They made calalú that you ate almost like yonyó. Yonyó was like a gumbo. It was prepared with wild amaranth and all sorts of spices. It was delicious, well seasoned. Okra tasted best when you ate it with your fingers. They also ate guengueré that was made with a tiny leaf of guengueré, beef, and rice. There were two classes of guengueré, the white and a purplish one. But the tastiest was the white on account of it was smoother.

They also ate masango which was boiled corn. I think the Congos ate it the same way.

Chequeté was the santeros' main drink. They always served it at their fiestas. It was like cold chocolate. They made it with oranges and vinegar. Children drank a lot of it. It was like atol that was made with sagú, arrowroot that was rolled and came out like corn starch. It was taken in spoonfuls, but a glutton would fill his cup all the way to the brim. But the most delicious of all those foods was ochinchín that was made with water cress, chard, almonds, and boiled shrimp. Ochinchín was the food of Ochún.

All the saints had their food. Obatalá had the black-eyed pea stew. And others I can't remember.

Many of those foods were harmful. Squash, for example, couldn't be eaten because there were saints that didn't get along with it. Even today a person doesn't eat squash. I myself wouldn't go into the woods to look for it because if you get tangled up in a patch of squash you break out all over. Your legs couldn't even support you for very long.

I didn't eat sesame seeds either because I got spots and pimples all over me. If the saints make an effort for you not to eat something, they have a good reason. Me, I don't even joke about that! Even now, I don't eat any of that, and it's not because the priest told me.

One should respect religions—even though you might not be much of a believer. In those days even the most clever man was a believer. The Spaniards were all believers. The proof is that on the feast days of San Diego and Santa Ana at Purio there was no work. The mill took a rest. The boilers were cold and the fields were deserted. It made you think of a sanctuary. The priests came in the morning and started to pray. They prayed for a long time. I learned little. I almost didn't even pay attention. And it's because I've never cared for priests. Some were criminals, even. They liked pretty white women and slept with them. They were both lecherous and pious. They had a child, and they called him a godchild or a nephew. They hid them under their robes. They never said, "This is my child."

They kept track of the blacks. If a woman gave birth, she had to call for the priest before the baby was three days old. If she didn't, a serious complaint was lodged with the owner of the mill. That was why all the children were Christians.

When a priest passed by, you had to say to him, "Your blessing, father." Sometimes they didn't even look at you. A lot of Spaniards and Canary Islanders are like that, not the Galicians.

Priests and lawyers were sacred in that period of time. They were highly respected because of their titles. Even a university degree was something special. Blacks were none of these things, least of all priests. I never seen a black priest. That was for the whites, and the descendants of the Spaniards. Even to be a night watchman you had to be Spanish. Though the only thing the nightwatchman is for is to keep watch. They earned six pesos a month. At Purio there was a fat one who was a Spaniard. He rang the bell for the faina and silence. He did nothing else. That was the most comfortable job in the world. I would have liked to be a night watchman. That was my ambition, but at Purio I never left the fields. That's why my arms were like masts. In spite of everything, the sun in the cane field is good. There's a reason I've lived so long.

Life itself in the sugarmills was tiresome. To see the same people and the same fields day after day was boring. The most difficult thing was to become used to the same place for a long time. I had to leave Purio because life there got to be a little dull. I set off walking south out of the hills. And I reached the San Agustín Ariosa central sugarmill, next to the town of Zulueta. At first I didn't want to stay because I preferred to keep walking. I was going to go on to Remedios, but it turned out that on that same plantation I took me a mistress, and I stayed. I liked that woman. She was pretty and bluish, one of those blue mulatas who doesn't care what people think. Her name was Ana. On her account I stayed to live there. But finally I got bored. That Ana frightened me with her witchcraft. Every night it was the same story, spirits and male witches. So I said to her, "I don't want to have any more to do with you, witch." She went on her way, and I never seen her again. Then I found another who was black, dark black like the earth. She was no witch, but she had a very positive nature. After two or three years being close to her, I left her. For my sake, she was trying too hard to be happy. But she wasn't the only one who could be happy. As soon as you came to a sugarmill to work, the women approached you. There was never a shortage of women who wanted to live with you.

I stayed at the Ariosa for a long time. When I arrived there the workers asked me, "Hey, where you come from?" And I told them, "I'm a freedman from Purio." Then they took me to the overseer. He gave me work. He put me to cutting cane. It didn't seem strange to me; I was already an expert at that. I also cleared the fields.

That sugarmill was average size. The owner was Ariosa by name, a pure blood Spaniard. The Ariosa was one of the first to be converted to a central because it had a wide belt that carried the cane to the boiler room. Inside there, it was like all other sugarmills. There were brown-noses and kiss-asses for the overseers and masters. They always questioned the new workers to find out what their opinions were. It was out of a hatred that has always existed between one group of blacks and another, out of ignorance. It can't be from anything else. And the freed slaves were very ignorant in general. They joined in on anything. There was even a situation where if an individual was a problem, his own fellow workers would kill him for a few gold coins.

The priests were influential in everything. When they said a black was bad tempered, you had to watch out for him because if you didn't, there was someone just waiting for the chance to cart him off.

At the Ariosa religion was important. There was a church close by, but I never went because I knew very well that the real founders of the Inquisition in Cuba were the priests, and I say this because the priests supported certain specific things...With women they were devils. They converted the sacristy into a whorehouse. Anyone who has lived at the Ariosa knows the stories. The stories got all the way to the barracoons. I know a good number of them. Other things I seen in person.

The priests put women in caves, in holes in the ground where they had executioners ready to kill them. Other caves were full of water, and the poor things drowned. I've been told that many times.

I seen priests with very racy women who later said, "Father, your blessing." And they went to bed with them. At the Ariosa there was talk of other matters, like how life was in the churches and the convents. The priests were like other men, but they had all the gold. And they didn't spend any. I never seen a priest having fun in a tavern. They closed themselves up in the churches, and that's how they passed the time. Every year they made collections for the church, for clothing, and for flowers for the saints.

It seems to me that the matter of the trapiches didn't attract their attention. They never went up close to the machines. They were afraid of choking or going deaf. Nobody else was so delicate.

In those years the machinery was run by stream. Myself, I went in one time to the trapiches, and as I approached the crusher I began to cough. I had to leave right away because my body wasn't accustomed to all that heat. The fields are different with their grasses and a dampness that clings to your skin.

The best job I had at the Ariosa was in the trapiche. Or near it, because it got me out of the fields. I really liked it. I had to dump the cane out of the conveyor belt. That was done inside near where a breeze still came in. The conveyor belt was the length of a palm tree. They brought the little wagon full of cane, and they backed it up to the conveyor belt. That was how it was unloaded. Four to six of us unloaded the cane from the wagons, and we went along putting it onto the conveyor belt. When the cane was all unloaded, the belt started moving along with ropes until it reached the crusher. The belt dumped the cane in the crushing room and then went back to get another load. You didn't waste any time in that work because the overseers were watching.

It was easy work. In the mixing room you worked easy, too. It was more enjoyable. There the thing was to fill up the little carts. There were some little carts that went empty up to the sugar boiler where they were filled with fresh sugar. When they were full, they were sent to the mixer. If the boilers were empty, they were scrubbed out with powerful jets of water. The mixer was a big machine with some hooks and a little trough where the sugar was deposited. The sugar was ground up in the mixer and sent as a solution to be refined in the centrifuge, which was a new machine at the Ariosa. Sometimes you didn't have to lift a finger for two days because the boilers would spill over every twenty-four hours. The whistle sounded with a noise that would deafen you. When the whistle went off, you had to be ready to gather the templa. Templa was what we called the stuff the boiler spilled over.

Those were the jobs I did at the Ariosa. I never fell asleep. If you fell asleep, you were punished, and if the overseer got really angry, he threw you out on your ear. When night came, I went to the barracoon and fell asleep immediately. I don't know what is more tiring, the woods, the trapiches...

During that period, I dreamt a lot, but I never dreamt in visions. Dreaming comes through the imagination. If you begin to think a lot about a particular banana grove, and you look at it, tomorrow or the day after you will dream about it. I dreamt about work and women. Work is bad for dreaming. It frightens you, and later, the next day, you think you're still dreaming, and that's when you get a finger caught in the machines or you slip.

Women are the ones who are really good at dreaming. I was mixed up with a dark Mooress, who wouldn't get out of my dreams. With that chick I spent all my time tangled up in strange things. She paid me no mind. I still remember her frequently. And I recall Mamá. Mamá was a old black woman, more or less a spy she was. She would go into the men's quarters, and say, "Good afternoon to you all." She would look around good, and then go and tell the overseer what she had seen. Bitch and betrayer. Everybody was afraid of her on account of her loose tongue. She had several mulatto children. She never mentioned the father. In my opinion it was the overseer. They always put her to doing light work. She served food and washed clothes, shirts, pants, and children's mamelucos. Mamelucos were little pants made of canvas with a couple of straps over the shoulders to hold them up. Little boys in those years wore nothing but those clothes. They were brought up like savages. The only thing they were taught was hoeing and sowing 'taters. Education, nothing. They were given the strap, and lots of it. Later on, if they kept on making mistakes, they were made to kneel down on grains of corn or salt. A whipping was the most frequent punishment. The parents would come with a switch or with the end of a rope, and they would give it to them till they drew blood. The switch was a thin branch of a tree that never split even though the child's skin would come away in strips. I think I had children. Probably many or maybe not. I don't think I would ever punish them that way.

In the market they sold lashes made of twisted rawhide. Mothers would tie it at their waist, and if the child began to misbehave, they let him have it anywhere at all. Those were beastly punishments inherited from slavery. Children nowadays are much more trouble. Before, they were quiet and really didn't deserve such punishment. Nowadays they are spanked instead of whipped. A child of that time spent the day running around in the bateyes or playing Spanish marbles. Little crystal marbles of all different colors. They were also sold in the markets. Two teams of six or ten boys played. They would make two lines in the dirt and take turns throwing the marbles. The one whose marble fell closest to the line won. Then they threw again, and if it touched a marble from the other team, they scored points.

They also played tejo, and the girls entertained themselves making rag dolls or playing rings with the boys. The boys dropped the ring in the hands of the girl they liked the most. They spent hours like that. Above all in the evening from six to eight or nine when they went to sleep. At the Ariosa they rang silence at the same hour as before, on the stroke of nine.

Every once in a while, there were children who ran away. They would beg for food at the houses so they didn't have to work. And they hid out. Many times they did it while running away from work or a licking from their own parents. Even during those years children didn't receive Christian instruction. But some parents had inherited that obsession and took them to church. Church was very important to the Spanish. They instructed the blacks in it everyday. But neither the Fabás or I ever went. The Fabás were both of them witches. One was called Lucas, and the other Ricardo or Regino. I was friends with Lucas. They had been slaves at the Santa Susana sugarmill, which was between Lajas and Santo Domingo. That sugarmill belonged to Count Moré. Lucas talked about that count a great deal. He said he was one of the cruelest Spaniards he had ever known. He didn't care for anybody. He gave orders, and you had to obey them. Even the governors feared him. Once Governor Salamanca [11] ordered him arrested because he paid the blacks with chits stamped with the T of the Holy Trinity. The count took money in gold and silver and paid with bits of paper. He was a strong-arm bandit. But the King of Spain heard about that problem and sent the governor to investigate it fully. So Salamanca went to the sugarmill in disguise. He arrived and sat down to eat in the mill tavern. No one knew he was the governor. He noted everything down in a little book, and when he found out the horrible things the count did, he sent for him, and said, "Come to the Governor's House." Moré replied, "It's the same distance from your house to mine. You come here." But Salamanca didn't go. He sent the Civil Guard instead, and they brought the Count in handcuffs to Havana. They put him in jail, and in a few months he died there. So, the counts, and viscounts looked for a way to get even with the governor. They became friendly with Salamanca's doctor so he would poison the governor, and Salamanca was poisoned in the year 1890 due to a growth he had on his leg. Instead of curing him, the doctor gave him poison, and he died in a few days. Lucas told me this because he saw it. It was the same year he arrived at the Ariosa with Regino.

Lucas was a big witch, and he really loved maní. He was a good dancer. He always said to me, "How come you no learn to dance maní?" and I said to him, "No, because the man who hits me will get a taste of my machete." Lucas knew a lot. He was a terrific guy. He danced maní to have a passel of women. Women liked men to be dancers. When a man was a good maní dancer, the women said, "Damn, I like that man!" and they took him to the bushes to have a good time because the toasty warm cane straw felt real good in cold weather. That business of going to the fields was well known. One would take advantage of the wagon ride from the mill to the cutting field. In the time it took, you could grab any woman at all and go off with her into the cane. You didn't have to make so many arrangements like now. When a woman went with you, she already knew that she would have to lay herself down on the ground.

Lucas was a good man, but he liked women too much. At times he and I used to get a group together to play monte at night in the barracoon. We would put a tarp down on the ground and sit on it to play. We played right through the night. But I quit when I saw that I had won four or five pesos, and if I was losing a lot, I would beat it out of there. I wasn't like those guys who play all night showing off just to lose. Besides, the games always ended badly because there were always arguments. Men are very selfish. It has always been like that, and if someone was losing and didn't think he should be, all hell broke loose. Since I've always minded my own business, I would leave.

At the Ariosa there were two black men who knew me as a boy. One day they said to Lucas, "He lived like a dog in the woods," and I saw them later and said to them, "Listen, the ones who lived like dogs were all you who got the whip," and the thing is that all those people who didn't run away thought the cimarrones were animals. There have always been ignorant people in the world. To know something, you have to be looking at it. I don't know what a sugarmill looks like inside unless I look at it. That's what happened to them. Lucas agreed with me because he knew me well. He was my only true friend.

At the Ariosa they didn't give work to just anybody. If they saw a natty man wearing a little woven hat, they didn't take him seriously because they said he was a dandy. To get work, it was better to go to those sugarmills looking a little raggedy with a palm or jipijapa hat. The overseers said that a dandy had no liking for busting his back, and at the Ariosa you had to work hard. They watched you all the time. They wrote you up for the least little thing. I remember a criminal by the name of Camilo Polavieja. Polavieja was the governor during the 90s. Nobody cared for him. He said that workers were oxen. He had the same attitude as during slavery. Once he ordered workers who didn't have identity cards to be given the componte. The identity card was a little piece of paper, like a pass, where the worker's address was written. You always had to have it on you, and if you didn't, you got some good licks on the back with a pizzle, a dried bull's cock. That was the componte. They always administered it in the police headquarters because that's where they took you if you didn't have a card. They cost twenty-five cents and had to be gotten at the Town Hall. They had to be renewed every year.

Besides the componte, Polavieja committed other atrocities. He beat blacks down by the thousands. He was as arrogant as a bull. He was even that way with his troops. The soldiers themselves said so. One time he decided to send blacks to the island of Fernando Po. That was a severe punishment because the island was deserted. It was a place for crocodiles and sharks. They let the blacks loose, and there was no escape. Thieves, pimps, cattle rustlers, and rebels were sent to Fernando Po. Any man who had a tattoo they shipped off. It was understood that a tattoo was a sign of rebellion against the Spanish government. The ñáñigos were also sent to that island and to others called Ceuta and Chafarinas. Polavieja sent the ñáñigos because he said they were anarchists. Workers who weren't involved in the ñáñigo movement or in the revolution remained in Cuba. Women weren't sent either. Those islands were only for men.

Polavieja made black women carry a little passbook. The passbook was similar to the identity card. They gave all the black women one of them in the Town Hall. That was their identification.

In those days women received a good deal of medical attention. A doctor went right to the Ariosa every Monday to examine them. A nobody Spanish doctor, a slipshod one. No one trusted the Spanish doctors. Witchcraft was what continued to make people well. Witches and Chinese doctors were the most in demand. Around here there was a doctor from Canton called Chin. Chin went around the countryside treating people who had money. I was in the town of Jicotea once, and I seen it. I never forgot it. The Madrazos, a family with money, brought him there. Chin was plump and short. He wore a light yellow doctor's smock and a little straw hat. Poor people only saw him from a long way off because he charged a lot. I've no doubt that he healed folks with those same herbs they put in bottles and sold in the pharmacy.

In Cuba there were many Chinese. They were the ones who had come as indentured workers. With time they got old and left the fields. Since I would often get away from the mill, I seen quite a bit of them. Above all in Sagua la Grande, which was their stomping grounds. Lots of workers went to Sagua on Sundays. They gathered there from all the sugarmills. That was how come I saw Chinese theater. It was a big theater made of wood, and well-constructed. The Chinese took great pleasure in things and painted with very bright colors. In that theater they did acrobatics and climbed up on each other's shoulders, one on top of the other. People clapped their hands a lot, and the Chinese bowed gracefully. The Chinese were the most refined thing in Cuba. They did everything silent and bowing.

In Sagua la Grande they had their own clubs. They gathered there to speak their languages and read newspapers from China out loud. They probably did it to be annoying, but since nobody could understand them, they kept right on with their reading as if nothing else mattered.

The Chinese were good at business. Their stores sold great numbers of strange things. They sold paper dolls for children, perfumes, and fabrics. The whole of Tacón Street in Sagua la Grande was Chinese. They also had tailor shops, candy shops, and opium dens there. The Chinese liked opium a lot. I think they didn't know it was harmful. They smoked it in long wooden pipes, hidden away in their shops so the whites and blacks couldn't see them—even though in those days they didn't go after anyone for smoking opium.

Another thing they really enjoyed was gambling. The greatest inventors of games were and are the Chinese. They played in the streets and in the doorways. I remember a game they called the button, and another which we still play now—charades. Blacks and whites went to Sagua la Grande to gamble with them. I didn't play anything but monte.

The Chinese would rent a house, and they got together in it on fiesta days. They gambled there until they dropped. They had a doorman in those houses to attend to the gamblers and to prevent fights. The doorman wouldn't allow any bullies to come in.

Whenever I could, I went to Sagua. Either by train or on foot—but almost always on foot because the train was very expensive. I knew the Chinese had fiestas on the important religious days. The town filled up with people to watch them celebrate. They did another trick where one of them lay on the ground with a millstone on his belly. Another Chinese picked up a sledge hammer and gave him a blow, and his belly was unhurt. Then, the Chinese man sat up, jumped to his feet, laughed, and the audience began to shout, "More!" Others, like the puppeteers in Remedios, burned papers and

dropped them on the ground. When the paper was burned
to ash, they poked around and pulled colored ribbons out of
the ashes. That's absolutely true because I've been told about
it many times. I know the Chinese hypnotized their
audiences. They've always had that ability. It's the
foundation of the Chinese religion.

Later they took to selling 'taters and fruits, and they
were ruined. Those happy times during Spanish rule have
been lost for the Chinese. Now you see a Chinaman, and you
ask him, "Am I doing all right?" and he says, "I not know."

Although I stayed several years at the Ariosa, things have
gotten a little blurry on me. The best thing for memory is
time. Time preserves the memories. When you try to
remember something from more recent times, you can't. On
the other hand, the farther back you look into the past, the
clearer you see it all. At the Ariosa there were lots of workers.
I think it was one of the biggest sugarmills in those days.
Everybody spoke well of it. The owner was an innovator, and
he made many changes in the trapiches. Some sugarmills
served very bad food because the company grocers didn't
care about the food. At the Ariosa it was different. There you
could eat. If the grocers weren't careful about the food, the
owner came and told them to take greater care. There were
sugarmills that operated the same as during slavery. The
thing was that the owners believed they were still slave
masters. That was often true in the sugarmills far from the
towns. When the fallow season came, the quiet time came,
too. The whole situation in the sugarmill and in the batey
changed. But everyone had something to do. The fallow
season was long, and the ones who didn't work, didn't eat.
You had to keep on doing something.

I gave myself up to looking for women in those months,
and I walked around through the towns. But I went back to

the barracoons at night. I could go to Sagua la Grande, to Zulueta, and to Rodrigo on the train. I went, but I didn't want to meet lots of people in those towns. So, in fact, my life was the sugarmill. What I did during the fallow season was hoe weeds because that's what I knew best. A couple of times I went to doing the edges which was hoeing weeds just as usual but on the boundary path between properties so that the cane didn't burn if there was a fire. New cane had to be planted, too, and you had to turn the earth over good so the plants would take hold. The cane was hilled over with a single ox and a little yoke. The ox went in between the cane rows. The plow was pushed by a farmhand. A lead boy eight or nine years-old guided the ox so he wouldn't slip off the furrow.

In the fallow season there were fewer duties and less work. Naturally, it could get very boring. Myself, I went into town when I had a few centavos. If not, what in hell was I going to find to do anywhere? In that case it was better to stay in the barracoon.

Women kept right on with their work. For them there was no fallow season. They went on washing the men's clothes, mending, and sewing. Women in those days were harder workers than women today.

Women didn't experience the fallow season. Their lives were spent raising chickens or pigs. There were still conucos but only in a few places. It seems to me that with freedom, the blacks no longer bothered with the conucos. The ones who kept theirs spent the off-season tending to it. I never had a conuco because I never had a family.

Another very common thing were the gamecocks, the raising of cocks for fighting. The sugarmill owners had that passion from way back. It wasn't just an obsession, it was almost a vice. They loved gamecocks more than people.

In the fallow season there were workers, blacks and whites, who spent their time taking care of the owner's gamecocks. The tenant farmers also had their little gamecocks, but they weren't rich enough to keep the expensive birds, the pedigreed ones. Gamecock breeders won a great deal of money in bets. They would bet eight or ten ounces of gold on a cock spur. If the cock was wounded in a fight, the keeper had to treat it immediately. He had to know the cocks well because they were pretty delicate. Sometimes, during a fight, a cock got hurt so bad that they picked him up half dead. Then they had to blow into his beak to clear out the blood clots and revive him again. He was thrown back into the ring, and as long as he was fighting he hadn't lost. To lose, the cock had to run away or drop dead. That was the only ending possible.

I often went to the cock fights in the pits around Ariosa. I liked to go to them although I've always thought it was cruel. I remember that I used to go to the cock pits with a clay pipe I bought at the mill store. I think it cost me a half peso more or less. I filled it with a plug of tobacco, and I set to smoking it to pass the time. The only ones who got bored were the ones who wanted the great hustle and bustle of fiestas and carnivals.

In the old days any slaves who died were buried in the sugarmill's cemetery. But after a few days you could hear voices, like groans, and you could see some white lights moving over the grave. That pile of dead people back then in the sugarmills brought out a great deal of witchcraft. For that reason, when slavery ended, they took the dead to town, to the big cemetery. The dead man's fellow workers carried him. Four of them carried him. They used two strong lengths of wild cane or palm. Each pole was held by two men in order to support the weight of the dead man. The sugarmill's carpenter made the coffin that was placed on top of the palm fronds. A box made of cheap, flimsy wood, pine wood. The candle holders were made of hollowed-out banana shoots. Four candles were put up, the same as now. Dead people were laid out right where they lived. If they lived in a cabin, they laid them out there—if not, in the barracoons.

Before, the custom of taking them to a funeral parlor didn't exist. On many occasions it happened that the dead came back to life. The thing is that they were buried too soon. Because of that they began waiting twenty-four hours to bury them. That's the modern system. Even so, it hasn't worked out because I've heard it said twenty times that there were dead men who, after being covered up with dirt, got up, skinny and sick, to go on screaming.

Right around here there was a cholera epidemic where one of those cases took place. All the people who looked pretty sick were carted off and buried. Later they got up as if nothing had happened. People were terrified.

When a worker died, the sugarmill filled up with people. Everybody came to pay their respects. There was camaraderie and reverence. A dead person, back then, was something very important. His family came on horseback from other sugarmills or faraway towns. Work didn't stop, but people were downhearted. When I learned about a death, I couldn't sit still.

The dead man was dressed up like a dandy, and they buried him that way. They laid him out in his best clothes. Even his rawhide shoes were forced onto his feet. On that day there was plenty of food. In the afternoon they served greens, rice, pork, almond drinks and brand T. beer. At night, white farmer cheese and yellow Spanish cheese were served. They also served coffee every few minutes. Coffee the way I like it. The only kind that tastes good. In cups of wild gourd that were grown only for that purpose.

If the dead man had relatives, they took care of the preparations. If not, his friends and their wives got together and did what was needed. When the dead man's family was refined, they served coffee in large cups. After everyone had eaten and talked, they took the body to the grave without any fuss, to the main cemetery, and I still maintain the thing is not to die because within a few days nobody remembers you, not even your best friends. The best thing is not to make such a fuss over the dead, as they do now, because the truth is that it's all hypocrisy. It was then and it is now. Give me the fiesta while I'm still alive.

The most curious thing during that time was falling in love. When a young man courted a young woman, he used a thousand tricks. You didn't do things so out in the open as now. There was mystery and trickery of all kinds. Myself, to attract a decent woman, I would dress all in white and pass by her without looking at her. I would do that for a few days. Until I decided to ask her something. Women like to see men dressed in white. A black man like me, in white, stood out. A hat was the handiest article of clothing because you could make a thousand gestures with it. You put it on, took it off, said hello to the women, asked them, "Say, how are you doing?"

The couple, if they had parents, especially the young women, could be made to fall in love by using grains of corn or pebbles. She would be on the porch of the cabin, and he passed by and said to her, "Pss, pss..." or whistled. When she looked, he smiled and tossed her the pebbles one by one. She replied by gathering up the pebbles and keeping them. If she didn't keep them, it was a sign that she didn't like him. That kind of a woman, block-headed and self-centered, probably gave the pebbles back.

The couple would see each other afterwards at a wake or a farm, at some fiesta or during the carnivals. If she had accepted his advances, she would say to him, "Listen, look here, I have these kernels of corn you threw to me." Then he would take her hand or kiss her. She would ask, "Are you going to come to my house?" He would tell her yes and leave. The next day he was at the house speaking to her parents. She would pretend, because that's the way of women, not to know him, and then say, "I'm going to think it over, Mr. Jones." Days before the wedding the house would be already fixed up. The bride's mother helped out in the hustle and bustle. They would have already gotten a dozen little stools, a big bed, a steamer trunk, and the cooking utensils. The poor didn't know about wardrobes The rich had them, but without mirrors. Wardrobes as big as horses made of cedar.

It was the custom for bride's parents and the godparents to give the groom a half dozen chickens, a big sow, a calf, a milk cow, and the wedding dress, which had a train because a person wasn't supposed to see the woman's ankles. The woman who showed her ankle wasn't religious or respectable. The man was the one who maintained the home, the boss of the house. She took orders and at first didn't work, except for a little washing for some other family. After they were settled, living in their house, they began to receive guests and to talk about the wedding party and the sweets and the beer. Everyday, in the morning, her mother or her old man would come to take a turn around the house. That was an obligation.

The priest could also come to visit—though the priests were more concerned with calling on the rich. What those saintly types were looking for was a handout. When a person was going to be married, he had to pay some six or seven pesos. Rich and poor alike. The poor, the sugarmill workers, were married in the chapel. The chapel was in the back, and the rich were married in the church, in the center, down the aisle to the main altar. They had pews and cushions there while the poor sat on wooden stools they had in the chapel, or sacristy, as it was called.

Generally, guests didn't enter the chapel. They stayed outside and waited for the newlyweds to come out. For the man who married a widow, they played a conch shell, and they banged old tin cans in his face to poke fun at him. They did that because the widower, as they called him, was like a mason. He was filling up a hole made by another. The more angry the man's reaction, the more cans and horns were sounded. If he said, "All right boys, let's drink," then they shut up and accepted the invitation. That was what experienced men did. But if one of those young oafs who didn't know a thing about life fell in love with a widow, he would get so furious you'd thing he was a savage. That was a good way to be despised by your buddies.

Having a good character is important in everything. When a person lives alone, it isn't necessary. But since we're always surrounded by people, the best thing is to be agreeable, not unpleasant. Those widows were quite shameless. There was one at the Ariosa who married a man from there. When they began to play the conch shell for him, she got embarrassed and hid her face. She was pretending. One day she went with a different man into the bushes, and they were caught. When she returned, nobody was friends with her.

Informal marriages worked out better. The women were free and didn't have to reckon with their parents. They worked in the fields. They helped with the hoeing or the planting, and they took up with you when they wanted to. Easy going men always took to that type of marriage. One today, a different one tomorrow. I think that's the better way. I always went around unattached. I didn't get married until after I was old. I was a bachelor in a lot of places. I met women of all colors. Arrogant ones and kind ones. In Santa Clara I had an old black woman after the war. She had so many illusions about me...She even asked me to marry her. I gave her a flat no. It's true that we got together, and she used to tell me, "I want you to inherit my house." She owned a big house with many rooms in the Condado section on San Cristóbal street.

A few days before she died she called me and told me that I was going to get everything. She filled out a document to leave me the Cabildo. In those years the house was a Cabildo Lucumí because her mother had been a famous santera in Santa Clara. When she died I went to claim the property. Then I found myself in a big kettle of fish. It turned out that her godfather wanted to get his hands on the house. He did that to me because the woman he had then lived in the house. She was the one who took care of the Cabildo. But when I found out about that scheme, I went quick, and fixed it all up. I went to some friends I had in the Provincial government. In the end I kept the house. It was bigger than I figured. Not a soul could live in it. Much less alone. It was a house full of spirits and dead folks. It was haunted. I sold it to a certain Enrique Obregón who used to be a loan shark. Later I traveled around with the money. I spent it all on saucy women. That happened after the war when I was already getting along in years.

If I count all the women I had at the Ariosa, I would have had a great many children. Well, I never met any. Anyhow, the women who lived with me in the barracoon never once gave birth. The others, the women I had in the woods, they came to me, and said, "This is your child." But who could be sure about that? Besides, children were a big problem in those times. They couldn't get learning because they didn't have the schools there are today.

When a child was born you had to take him to the courthouse within three days to have him recorded. The first thing was to give the skin color. Babies were born without any trouble. The women then didn't have the labors that the women have today. Any old country woman was a better midwife than the ones who train for it today. I never seen a child die on one of them. They poured alcohol on their hands and pulled the babies out and cut their umbilical cords, which healed up right away. Those old women, midwives, divined the day and the hour that a woman was going to give birth, and they were part curanderas, too. Indigestion they cured in the blink of an eye. They cured it with a cow patty. They collected it dry and boiled it. They strained it in a fine piece of cloth, and after two or three doses the indigestion disappeared. They cured all kinds of sicknesses. If the child got gingivitis, which was a bad disease of the gums, they gathered wild grasses from the woods, they crushed them, and then they made a tea of them and gave it to him. That killed the infection immediately. Doctors today give different names to these diseases. They call them infections or rashes, and it turns out that it takes longer to cure them than before when we had no injections, or x-rays, either.

Medicine was herbs. Nature is full of remedies. Any plant can be a curative. The only thing is that many haven't been discovered yet. I want to know why doctors don't go to the countryside to experiment with plants. It seems to me that they are such good businessmen that they don't want to just come out and say that such and such a leaf will cure you. Then they fool you with prepared medicines that in the end are very expensive and don't cure anybody. Back then, I couldn't buy those medicines, and therefore I didn't go to the doctor. A man who earned twenty-four pesos a month couldn't spend even a centavo on a bottle of medicine.

At the Ariosa I earned twenty-four pesos, though at some point, I think they were paying me twenty-five, like at Purio. The thing about the pay was that it was flexible. It depended on how the man was on the job. I was a good worker, and they were finally paying me twenty-five. But there were poor souls who kept on earning twenty-four, and even eighteen pesos a month. The pay included food and rooming in the barracoon. That didn't change my mind. I was always clear that that life was good for animals. We lived like pigs, and so no one wanted to make a home or have children. It was too hard thinking that they were going to suffer the same hardships.

There was a lot of activity at the Ariosa. Every now and then technical advisers would come. They would look around the fields, and then they would go to the boiler house. They looked at the functioning of the sugarmill to eliminate the trouble spots. When some visitor was announced, the overseer ordered people to put on clean clothes and to make the boiler house shine like the sun. Even the foul odor disappeared.

The technical advisers were foreigners. At that time Englishmen and Americans were already coming here. The machines had been steam driven for many years. At first they were small machines. Later on, other, bigger ones arrived. The small machines were removed because they were very slow. Those machines had no shredders, and they didn't remove all the juice from the cane. In the old trapiches, half the guarapo went out with the bagazo. They were quite useless. The most important equipment was the centrifuge. That machine had been in use around here for some forty years. I came across it when I first arrived at the Ariosa. Now, there are sugarmills that still don't have one, like the Carmelo, the Juanita, and San Rafael.

The centrifuge is a round tube where the molasses drips down so the sugar remains dry. If a sugarmill didn't have a centrifuge, it had to make muscovado, brown sugar, which is a mixed sugar. The drink that could be made from that sugar was very good. It was as filling as a steak. The big machine at the Ariosa had three rollers. They were the shredder, the crusher, and the extractor. Each one had a function. The shredder did nothing but break up the cane. The crusher squeezed the sugar out to make guarapo, and the grinder left the bagazo dry and ready to be taken to the furnaces to make steam. The men who worked those machines had the best job in the mill. They figured they were better than the rest. They looked down on the field hands. They said the cane cutters were cuerós, which meant something like "crude." They spent a lot of their time making fun of them. If the cutters had calluses on their hands, they said to them, "Hey, look out, you're going to scratch me," and they wouldn't shake hands with them for anything in the world. They created a very destructive way of thinking. They sowed hate and separateness. They slept separate from everybody else. Likewise the machinists, the crystallizing pan operators, the sugarmasters, the weighers. They all had their houses in the batey, and quite comfortable ones, too. Some were cement although at the Ariosa there were still many of the wooden houses with little decorations on the roof. The way those men acted was wrong. Later on, they recognized things were changing, and they tried to be different. But for me it seemed that the guy who worked out in the sun always got the worst deal. He was the one who sacrificed the most, and he was the one most beaten down. He had to stay in the barracoons every night.

The truth is that progress is amazing. When I saw those machines moving all at once, I was impressed, and to tell the truth, they seemed to go by themselves. I never before had seen so much progress. The machines were English and American. I never seen a one from Spain. They didn't know how to make them. The tenant cane farmers were the most excited about the new things. They were happier than anybody else because more production in the boiler house meant that more cane was bought from them by the mill.

The tenant farmers were still a recent development in that period. You can't say they had large plantings of cane. A small landholder had his little field of ten or fifteen besanas sown to cane. Sometimes they were pushy, and planted cane right up to the edges of the batey, twenty-five to thirty feet away. The tenant farmers were a bunch of sourpusses even so. They didn't have enough land to become rich. That came later. They sure were mean sons of bitches. Meaner, and stingier than the plantation owners themselves. The tenant farmers overworked the soil. They nagged the workers every day, and they were more watchful than the sugarmill owners. If there was a piece of land that cost forty pesos to work, they paid twenty, half, that is, and at times you had to put up with it because they had their cohorts. Even though they didn't get along with each other. The workers almost never had any dealings with the tenant farmers. They went to the fields and all, but nobody had anything to do with them. To get paid they had to go to the storekeeper. It was better that way. During that period of time, the tenant farmers were a bunch of deadbeats, almost all of them, so they couldn't pay a mayordomo. They began to get bigger later, when the price of sugar went up. Some of them got to be powerful. The sugar cane fever arrived, and they left hardly any forest in Cuba. Trees were cut down at the roots. They took out mahoganies, cedars, indigo trees. Well, the whole forest was chopped down. That was after Independence. Now, if a person goes up to the north of Las Villas he will probably say, "There is no forest around here." But when I was a cimarrón, a person could be scared there. It was thick like a jungle.

Cane was grown, but it destroyed the beauty of the country. The ones to blame were the tenant farmers. Tenant farmers were almost without exception bad people. Maybe only Baldomero Bracera could be excluded. He started a tenant farm with the name of Juncalito in the marsh land of the Yaguajay valley. He drained the whole piece in a short time. That gave him a lot of prestige, and he became important. He had more credit than a guy named Febles, the owner of the Narcisa mill, where Baldomero's farm was. Febles sure was a tyrant. He would start throwing punches for nothing at all. He paid very poorly. One day a worker went to him and said, "Pay me." Febles ordered him to be thrown in the furnace. The man was burned to a crisp. There was nothing left but chittlings, and that was how the crime was discovered. They didn't even touch Febles. That's why when you had a man like Baldomero, people loved and respected him. If he had to fire someone he told him to his face. One of the most important things Baldomero did was to bring a cane hauling machine to the Narcisa. Other mills already had them but not the Narcisa because Febles didn't have enough credit. So Baldomero lent him the money and sent off for the machine. I seen it, and I remember it because it had a big number one painted on it. Baldomero was a no-nonsense farmer. A good businessman. He used his brains to run his business. He gave money for public works and for commerce. He paid decent wages. The town of Yaguajay deeply mourned the death of that man. I never worked for him, because I was at the Ariosa, but I seen him and heard many accounts of his life and his rise in society. Baldomero was the exception.

You can't imagine what a tinderbox those years were. People spent all their time talking about uprisings. The war was approaching. But to my mind people still weren't sure when it was going to start. Many said that time was running out for Spain. Others wouldn't open their yap, or they stuck their heads in the urinal. Myself, I didn't say anything though I liked the revolution and admired the men who were risking their lives. The most popular were the anarchists. They got orders from Spain, but they wanted Cuba to be free. They were something like the ñáñigos because they were very organized and had their contacts everywhere. They were real brave. People talked about them all the time. After the war, the anarchists took over in Cuba. I didn't follow them any more. What we didn't know about was the annexation that's being talked about now. What we wanted as Cubans was the freedom of Cuba. For the Spanish to go away and leave us alone. You didn't say anything but "Liberty or Death," or "Cuba Libre."

Many people were up in arms and looking for trouble with this business of independence. They went up into the hills and stayed there for a few days making an uproar. Then they came back down, or they were arrested. The Civil Guard was a hellish bunch. No one could mess around with them. Off with the head of anybody they arrested. We blacks protested, too. It was an old protest, years old. It seems to me that we blacks protested too little. I still maintain that belief. I remember the rebellion of the Rosales brothers—Panchito, and Antonio. One of them was a newspaperman and had a print shop in Sagua la Grande because they were from there. A rumor got started right off that the Rosales were brave and were attacking the Spanish government. From then on the town was with them. I became interested in them too. One day, while I was just passing through Sagua, I saw Francisco. As soon as I saw him, I realized he didn't give a damn He was elegant and impressive, but he would slit anybody's throat. Francisco was a horse thief and a bandit. I think he worked at barbering. Later I saw the two of them in Rodrigo. They went there frequently. They went to let off steam, of course. Those mulattoes got too big for their own britches. They passed themselves off as white. Come on! They shot Antonio in Sagua. The Spanish government arrested him, and they shot him, and that was the last you heard of them. Please don't try to tell me that they were revolutionaries. They fought hard, but they didn't know why. Well, neither did we know why, but we weren't bandits. The people at the Ariosa, at least, were decent and straightforward. Those who wanted to could become accomplices to the bandits and horse thieves. But that was according to each person's taste and the situation. Nobody obliged anybody to steal. Evil clings to whoever is evil. I was in the war with a handful of degenerates, and I came out real clean. To tell the truth, though, bandits weren't killers. If they had to kill someone, they killed him. But they weren't what you can call killers.

There were many bandits here before the war. Some became famous. They spent their time in the countryside, going after the people with money and the tenant farmers. Manuel García was the best known of all of them. Everyone around knew him, and there were people who said he was a revolutionary. I know about many other bandits. Among them, Morejón, Machín, Roberto Bermúdez, and Cayito Alvarez[12.] Cayito was a savage. Good-looking like nobody else. You can ask anybody in Las Villas about Cayito. He was in the war, too. Many lies have been said about him, all made up.

Morejón was a miserable wretch. He would rob a fortune, but he didn't follow the custom of Manuel, who gave food to the poor. I never heard that he gave money for the Revolution. Morejón was always in hiding. He was a bit of a coward and very cautious. He liked to steal. His whole life was banditry. Robbery was second nature to Morejón. He didn't create a fuss. I don't think he ever kidnapped anyone, but he would stop people on the road, and say to them, "Give me everything you've got on you." He took the centavos and left. I never heard of him threatening anybody. He seemed quiet, but he was a criminal.

Las Villas was the stomping grounds of the bandits. They swarmed all around there. All of them did kidnappings, from the best to the worst. Others had a the knack of stealing money quietly. North of Las Villas there were many well to do families. Agüero sacked almost all of them. He was the biggest thief of them all. He even took the chickens and the pigs. His little vice was to take everything. They say he went off yelling after he stole. They chased after him, and the rural guard would surround him, but he always had the ability to get away. Agüero would go into the sugarmills like he was at home. He used the trick of disguising himself because the bandits made themselves pass for lottery ticket vendors, for workers, and for rural guards. One time Agüero went into the Ariosa. They say that he pulled off a big job. I didn't see it. He walked slowly up to the place like a rural guard, and he was dressed like one. He asked for the owner of the mill. At the store they told him, "Go up there. The house isn't far." When he got to the Basque's house, he asked again, and they had him come inside. That was when Agüero cornered him and asked him for a large sum of money. The thing was that the Basque gave it all to him, never thinking it was Agüero the thief. That day he had on a good disguise and talked like a Spaniard. The first thing Agüero asked the Basque to do was to dismiss the guard, who wasn't needed, and being a fool the Basque said to the guard, "You may leave."

The gossips say that General Máximo Gómez himself took money from Agüero for the Revolution. I don't doubt it. The only one who never accepted money from bandits was Martí, the patriot from Tampa, the finest man in Cuba.[13]

The country folk were decent, and they were afraid of the bandits. That was why one of Agüero's sidekicks turned him in to the rural guard. It seems that they forced him to hand him over. That man's story was too much. His greed made him devour sugar plantations.

In Remedios one of the biggest kidnappings ever was of the Falcón family. That was one of the strangest families in Las Villas. They caused a whole lot of trouble. There was jealousy, hatred, hypocrisy in that family. All the things heartless people can think up. Among them there was one, Miguel Falcón, who didn't have a centavo. He was from Remedios. Don Miguel married a good woman. She didn't know what sort of man he was. She was the widow of the brother of Modesto Ruíz, who was then the mayor of the town. She was widowed when her daughters were already grown. Even so, don Miguel wanted to hook up with her because she was attractive and still young looking. Everybody called her Antoñica, though her real name was Antonia Romero. Her family was well thought of. All of Remedios respected them. But the fact is that during Polavieja's government, don Miguel planned the kidnapping of Modesto Ruíz.[14] Modesto wasn't so bad, but nobody could figure out why he had so much money. At that time a certain Mendez, who was Spanish, I think, was a lieutenant colonel of the voluntarios from Vueltas. Méndez had Polavieja's trust, and don Miguel knew it better than anybody. That was why he planned Modesto's kidnapping. What Polavieja didn't know was that Méndez was the leader of a gang of bandits and much less that Méndez himself was the most degenerate and the biggest bandit of them all.

One day don Miguel went to see him and said, "We have to get those 10,000 pesos from Modesto," and Méndez said to him, "Let's go!" So they rounded up two or three others and took advantage of the visits Modesto made to his estate La Panchita. On one of those trips they grabbed him and took him to the forest where they made him tell where he kept his money. Of course, don Miguel didn't show his face so Modesto wouldn't be able to recognize him. I think that Méndez's bloodthirsty bunch kept him a prisoner for two weeks. He told them right away about the money, and they carried it all off. They left Modesto locked up in a house with his feet tied. They even ordered a mulatto from the gang to kill him and bury him good, head and all. The mulatto went to see Modesto, and they talked. Modesto kept repeating to him, "If you let me go, I'll give you a reward." The mulatto, sort of feeling sorry for him, said, "I'll let you go if you promise to get me out of the country." Modesto said yes, and the mulatto untied him. The next day, Miguel Falcón found out about all of it and pretended to be happy. He put on a big feed at his house to welcome Modesto back. Modesto went and received all the fanfare. But the witch was loose, and Modesto said to himself that it wasn't going to end there.

He began to look into it fully, and when he had all the facts together, he went right to Polavieja. The murderer Méndez had already ordered the mulatto be killed so he didn't leave Cuba or any damn place. Polavieja, who hated the bandits, sent for Méndez, and gave him a court martial. Méndez was shot in the city of Havana. They jailed don Miguel for a few days, and then deported him to Ceuta, which was an island surrounded by devils. He died there a short while later. The truth came out, and everybody was shocked. No one could conceive of the schemes those bandits planned. Antonia, poor thing, was struck dumb. Above all when she found out that her own husband had tried to kill Modesto, her brother-in-law, so that her daughters would get the uncle's inheritance plus the 10,000 pesos that the gang was going to split up. I don't know if they caught the rest of the gang. It seems unlikely because the guard in those years was not as alert as it is today. They were blood-suckers, but stupid. Antonia Romero was a real woman. She was mortified, but she didn't let it break her spirit. Her daughters' spirits, either. When the war started, Antonia began to collaborate. She sewed clothes and cooked. She delivered medicines and went into the forest. She came to hold a revolutionary rank. She was a lieutenant colonel in the war of independence.

There are some who would have you believe the bandits were benefactors. They say they were noble because they robbed for the poor. It seems to me that stealing is stealing, no matter how you look at it, and the bandits didn't hesitate to rob anyone. A rich person or a somewhat rich person. For them the important thing was to have dough on them, and they never went without, that's for certain. At times they had to hide out in the house of a guajiro and eat their plate of sweet potatoes so as not to go hungry. That's where that phrase that bandits are benefactors comes from. Of course, if the guajiros offered them house and home, they had to pay with something. When they stole a pile, they went around and shared it. That was why the guajiros were such good friends of the bandits. They didn't become bandits, but they were their friends. The guajiros have always been accommodating. They would see a bandit on his horse, and the wife would say, "Come on in and have a sip of coffee." The bandit got down and took advantage of their trust to become friendly with the family. Those same bandits sometimes grabbed the young guajiras and carried them off. Those were the most common kinds of kidnappings. I still don't know anybody more woman-crazy than those jokers. They would risk everything to see a woman. The Civil Guard took advantage of visits they made to women and ambushed them right there. They hunted down many bandits that way because no one could catch them out in the countryside. They were the best riders and quick as lynxes. Besides, no one knew the woods as well. Many people said they were revolutionaries and wanted freedom for Cuba.

Others labeled them autonomists. All of that was just bragging. No murderer can be a patriot. Arsonists was what they were. They would go up to a farmer and ask him, "Say, where's the dough?" If the farmer said he wasn't giving anything, they threatened to burn his fields, and it was no joke. Sometimes, you would see a big fire, and it was their doing.

Their custom was to go out at night. All their dirty work took place then. They rested in the daytime. It was a dangerous life because the Spanish government hated them. This island was infested with bandits. They were in all the provinces.

The most popular of them was Manuel García, who they now call the king of the Cuban countryside. They even talk about him on the radio. I never ever seen him, but I know that he traveled all around. People tell lots of stories about him.

Manuel didn't miss a chance. Wherever he saw gold coins, that was his harvest. His bravery won him many friends and many enemies. More enemies than friends, I think. They say he was no murderer. I don't know. What is certain is that he had a guardian angel. Everything worked out well for him. He was friends with the guajiros, a true friend. When they saw the Civil Guard approaching where Manuel was, they took off their pants and hung them on a line with the belt down. That was the signal for Manuel to hightail it. That was why he lived so long as a bandit.

He was the most daring of them all. He would just as soon stop a train as derail it. He took protection money. How to tell it all...? It got to the point where Manuel didn't even cut the telegraph lines because he was so sure that no one was going to catch him. Salamanca and Polavieja fought him like nobody else. Another general who came here, by the name of Lachambre, was out to capture Manuel. But Manuel laughed at him and sent him letters threatening to hang him. Lachambre was sharp, but he could never find Manuel. And there was all that talk about how the Spanish had better weapons and more men.

Manuel García's gang used an eighteen-shot rifle. They were good, better at least than the blunderbusses the other bandits had. It was a well-equipped gang. They had cooks, aids, and all the rest. They were never without tobacco or hot chocolate or greens or pork.

Manuel García was very troublesome, above all in Havana. He liked his way of life, and he wasn't ashamed to say so. First he was a cattle thief in the forest, stealing oxen to sell. Then he moved on to stealing money and kidnapping people.

I think Manuel was born in Quivicán. It was there he married Rosario, who was his only wife. She was in prison on the Isle of Pines, and people had a lot to say about it. Vicente García,[15] Manuel's brother, was a bandit like him. I think he also belonged to his gang. But he wasn't so famous. I heard a lot of talk about Osma, who was Manuel's right hand man. A stubborn, black bastard who later went over to the Spanish partisans. He fought with those guerrillas in many places. In Las Villas there were many of them. Osma used to kill at point blank range with a big brass and wood blunderbuss. People talked about Osma as though he were a witch. It isn't clear to me. But I do believe there had to have been something like that going on because to travel like it did, his gang needed its special stick magic.

Manuel García never got to the War of Independence. Or rather, he never fought in it. He gave a great deal of money, that's certainly so. Some 50,000 pesos at least. Máximo Gómez took it like it had fallen out of the sky.

Garcia's death has remained somewhat murky. When a man is important like him, it's hard to know who killed him. Manuel had many enemies because he looked for trouble in every family he got mixed up with. He kidnapped a guy named Hoyo, and then his relatives went after Manuel. But no luck. Manuel knew the forest like the palm of his hand.

Many of the old timers who knew Manuel personally have told me that women were his perdition. But I know that they killed him for giving money to the Revolution. A traitor passing himself off as a revolutionary waited for him one day in the forest and told him to light his cigar to identify himself. Manuel, trusting him, went to the appointment as he promised. He was carrying thousands of pesos. As he approached, the traitor called out to the Civil Guard for them to shoot him, and they made sieve of him. That was how Manuel Garcia died.

Other people give the matter another twist. People from the western provinces say Manuel died because he went to see a broad in La Mocha. That he went every night to sleep with her. One day, the old fool went to the town priest and told him, "Ay, father, I have sinned with Manuel García," and the priest turned her over to the authorities. A few days later, Manuel went into that woman's house and opened the gate and left it like that. He came out in a short while, and the gate was shut. It seemed strange to him, and he was surprised. When he went to open it again, they shouted, "Manuel García!" He looked up, and the Civil Guard killed him right there.

I've heard the story yet another way. The sacristan of the parish of Canasí killed him in a store, and then Manuel's gang hacked the sacristan to pieces in the forest with machetes. It's all difficult, and no one can say what the truth is. As with Maceo's death, there's more than meets the eye.

It's hard for people to say things clearly. That's why I say that witches will be witches and all, but they can't keep the truth quiet. They tell you who your enemy is, and how you can get rid of him. At the Ariosa, the only ones to speak clearly were witches, and if you paid them, even more so. Many people were afraid of them. They took to saying that they ate children, that they took your heart out, and a heap of junk more. When you hear about all that, you shouldn't be frightened. You should investigate it all. Those who talk like that have something eating at them.

I'm not a supporter of witchcraft, but neither do I talk foolishness just for pleasure. I'm more afraid of other things than I am of witchcraft. I wasn't even afraid of the bandits. Also I was poor, really busted, and no one was going to kidnap me, and you wouldn't believe how much I walked. I walked around till I got worn out.

The forests tire out you when you're in them every day. Even more when you work from sunup to sundown. Because that old sun gets stuck in the sky and bears down on you. In the daylight, when I was in the cane field, the sun went through my shirt and burned me through and through. The heat was brutal.

I sweated all over. Anyway, when you go walking, the sun seems more noble. It cools down a little, or it seems to you that it cools down.

But going back to the thing about fear. Fear of witches. That's silly, and fear of bandits is, too. What was very serious, and everyone was in agreement about this, was the Spanish police and the Captains of the Partido. While at the Ariosa, I remember a captain who was a real fireball. I can't recall his name, but the fact is that without knowing it, he could really get to you. Just saying "Here comes Captain of the Partido" was enough. Well, that was like saying, "Here comes the devil." Everyone ran away from the captains. If they saw some problem or only caught a whiff of something, they would try to catch you. When the blacks began to turn against Spain, those captains had a grand time. A black revolutionary was not to be allowed. They would kill him on the spot. Still, if he was white, well...I know it's better not to remember that time. There is nothing worse than a Spanish blockhead's whip and to have to keep your trap shut!

Whoever behaved in an unacceptable way would be sent to clean out the Civil Guard's stables. The guard always traveled on horseback although some of them did service in the infantry. The ones who had horses were tougher. There were none of those little, short men in the Civil Guard, hell no, they had none of that, and they didn't have any good men either. They were all a bad bunch. They lasted so long because it appears that in those days not as many men were rebels, like now. Back then, a revolutionary was a rare thing. People were too long-suffering, more than the average. No one was capable of standing up to a captain. They would die first.

There was a reddish black man who made a name for himself in Cuba. He was called Tajó. He lived at Sapo. This Tajó guy one day disarmed two pairs of Civil Guards at the same time. He was always outside the law. An escaped prisoner and a mugger until the war began. Tajó was a wild dog. He carried off any woman he liked, and woe to you if you complained. If by some chance the father of the woman came to take her back, Tajó pulled out his machete to scare him off, and the poor man would run away. That's how evil he was. He always had his way. He laid his own daughters. Everybody was aware of that though they did nothing about it. His poor daughters spent their entire lives in the house and didn't even go outside to sit in the sun. They looked like ghosts from being shut in so much. At the small farms, people didn't know what they looked like, whether they were pretty or ugly, nothing. He wanted them for his personal pleasure, nothing more. I never seen those girls. I know it's true because everyone told the story. News came to the Ariosa like foam on the water. There were some who said that after screwing the females in the towns around there, Tajó killed them and buried them in an ant hill. That's an exaggeration though I would believe just about anything about that son of a bitch. His pastimes were criminal. The type of man who didn't think of having fun or playing games, either. He thought of nothing but doing harm. In the war I had to obey his orders. The fault of Máximo Gómez, the one who named him head of a squadron.

Going back to women. It's true that they were the main topic of conversation. Although in a different way. You would go to talk to your friends, or with acquaintances rather, and they would tell you what they did with women. I never was one to tell stories about my experiences. A man should learn to be reserved. Now, those blabbermouth men would tell you calmly, "Listen, José, you know that tomorrow I'm going to have me little Juanita," and if he was talking to me, I pretended not to hear anything, to keep my distance. I've never liked that kind of gossip. That's why I stick with gambling, which is a healthier entertainment.

At the Ariosa you could play dominoes with good players. Dominoes was a little hard to play. You had to have a clear head. We played "invitation" and "tin-tin-tin," where the tiles had to be turned spots down. If the guard caught you playing, the handful of whippings he gave out was a yessir, father! Since I got bored with the ins and outs of dominoes, I used to go to the batey or listened to the old timers and the young men when they got to telling about visions.

All men have visions, and most of them keep quiet about them. For me, visions are true and should be respected, not feared. I've seen many different ones. I've remembered some of them. Others have been told to me. Like the one of a friend of mine who had a glowing fire that came out of his right arm. It was dangerous because if it had come out the left arm, it would have surely meant he was going to die. There are some folks who think a great deal about visions, and they sit waiting, half-dizzy, for them to come. They don't come then. That's why many people don't believe in them.

Seers have visions almost every day. People who aren't seers can see them, too, but less frequently. I myself can't be called a seer though I've seen strange things. For example, a light that came out walking along beside me, and when it came to places where money was buried, it would stop to pick it up. Then it disappeared. Those were dead people who came out with the object of collecting money. Others came out in the form of lights. They did it on account of promises. They stuck by my side too, and they didn't tell me, but I knew that what they were looking for was for me to pay the church for a promise. I never obeyed that commandment, and the lights followed me regularly. They don't follow me any more because I don't get around much now, and those lights belong out in the country.

Another vision was the güijes. Holy mother, the güijes caused a big stir each time they came out. I never seen a one but blacks had a natural inclination for them. The güijes would come out in the rivers at all hours. When they sensed someone coming, they would hide, scrambling for the bank. They came out to sun themselves. They were dark little black things with the hands of a man, and feet...I never knew what their feet were like, but their head was flattened down like a frog's. Just like one. Mermaids were another vision. They came out in the sea. Above all at the feast of San Juan. They came up to comb their hair and to look for men. They were very flirty. There have been many cases of mermaids carrying men off, cases where they took them to the bottom of the ocean. They had a preference for fishermen. They took them down, and after keeping them there for a period of time, they would let them go. I don't know what potion they had so the men didn't drown. That's one of those strange things in life. That there are things that remain in the dark.

Witches were another of those rare things. At the Ariosa, I seen how they caught one. They trapped her with sesame seeds and mustard, and she stayed put. While there's a single sesame seed on the ground, witches can't move. To get away, witches would leave their skin behind. They would hang it behind the door and come out raw like that, in their meat. They are finished here because the Civil Guard wiped them out. I never seen any Cuban witches. They flew here every night. From the Canary Islands to Havana in a few seconds. Even today, when people are not so fearful, they leave a light on in houses where there are little children so that witches will not get inside. If not, that would be the end because they're very partial to children.

Another vision for real is the headless horsemen. Riders who ride out to mourn. They put a dreadful scare in you. One day I came across one, and he told me, "Go over there and dig up the gold." I went over, sort of trembling, and when I pulled my hands out, I had only coal. It was a dead jokester buried without a cross, and I curse his family a thousand times because he never came out again! Those ghosts were terrible. Afterwards, they say that the dead, well,...What do I know? All in all, they're more trouble than living folks.

In the mills there were all kinds of hexes. The Filipinos were always mixed up in the business with witches. They hung around blacks, and they even slept with black women and all. They were criminal. If one of them died, they buried him next to a black, and he came out after awhile with red clothes on to frighten people. These visions were more likely seen by old folks. Truth is that young people see very little. Even today, a young person isn't prepared to see things.

Young people didn't hear voices, either. The voices of the country. You would go along a path at night, and you would sense a shout or a snort. Since I was used to that, I didn't become really afraid. I was already primed to hear them. Right there, in Santa Clara, they said that in the runoff of the Alvarez' pigsty you could hear snoring at night. Heck, I was told that. I never seen those shapes. They have always seemed to me to be spirits who owed something, a mass or a prayer session, though other people may say the opposite. After they complete their mission, they disappear. Whoever peeks at them loses out.

All of that is spiritual, and you have to face up to it without being a coward. Living people are more dangerous. I've never heard it said that You-Know-Who's spirit set in on clubbing So-and-So. But how many living people are there who pull out each other's hair every day! That's the thing. It has to be understood that way. No other way. If a dead person comes up to you, don't run away, but ask, "What do you want, brother?" He will answer or take you someplace. Never turn your face away from them. You can't say they are our enemies, in the end.

People back then had a kind of fear of the dead. Even the Chinese were scared and opened their eyes wide. Their skin loosened up on them each time a fellow countryman died. All a man had to do was stretch out, and the Chinese took off, leaving him there alone. Alone, all alone. The dead man didn't say a word. What could he have said? When a few hours passed, they would get back together again, hire a Cuban to attend to him, and bury him. Then they went to his room, and I thought they were cooking because soon after a wonderful smell came out that wasn't opium. Myself, I can't explain why they were so scared. I don't know what caused it.

The Congos were distinctive in their ways. They weren't afraid of the dead. They became serious and quiet but had no fear. When a Congo died you couldn't cry. You had to pray a lot and sing real low, without drums. Then they took the dead man to the cemetery next to the mill and buried him without a coffin. Around there they had no boxes to put the dead in. Anyway, they didn't use them. I think it's better to go like that and not all closed up without being able to do anything in that darkness. There was a little mound in the place where they buried him, and on that mound they put a cedar wood cross so the man would have protection. The Congos said that a dead man shouldn't keep his eyes open. They closed them for him with sperm, and they stayed closed. If his eyes opened, it was a bad sign. They always placed him face upward. I don't know why but it appears to me it was the custom. They put shoes and everything on the dead. If he was a palero he had to leave his prenda to someone. Usually when one of those Africans got sick, he made it known who would inherit it. Then the prenda remained in the hands of that person. Now, if that person couldn't carry on with the inherited prenda, he had to throw it in the river so the current would carry it off. Because anyone who didn't understand about an inherited prenda would have his life all screwed up. Those prendas could rebel on you like a son of bitch. They could kill anyone.

To prepare a prenda that works well, you have to gather rocks, sticks, and bones. Those are the main things. When lightning strikes, the Congo mark the place well. Seven years went by, and they would return there, dig a little, and take out a smooth rock for the cazuela. Also the buzzard's stone was good for its power. You had to be prepared for the moment when the buzzard went to lay her eggs. She always laid two. You would carefully take one of them and boil it in salt water. After a short time you took it to the nest. It was left there until the other egg hatched its chick. Then the hard-boiled one, dry as it was, waited until the buzzard went to the sea. Because she thought that that egg would hatch a chick too. From the sea she brought some magic. That magic was a tiny rough stone that was put in the nest next to the egg. The tiny stone contained a very strong witch. After a few hours a chick came out of the hard-boiled egg. That was the honest truth. The prenda was prepared with that tiny stone. So this business was no game. One of those prendas couldn't be inherited by just anyone. That was the reason the Congos died so sad.

There are people who say that when a black dies he goes back to Africa. That's a lie. How would they go back to Africa? The ones who went back were alive, the ones who flew a lot—a tribe of wild men the Spanish refused to bring here anymore because it wasn't good business. But the dead don't fly! Though the Chinese did. They died here, at least that's what they say, and came back to life in Canton. What happened to the blacks, which is the same today as it was yesterday, is that the spirit went out of the body and set to wandering around in the ocean or in space. Like when a snail looses its shell. It goes into another shell, then another, and another. That's why there are so many shells. The dead don't leave as the dead; they leave in the shape of spirits. At the Ariosa one came out called What's-his-face Congo, I mean Faustino. He drank rum like a fish. He came out because he had money buried in clay pots. In the old days, they used to bury money that way. Banks didn't exist. Two Spaniards who were digging ditches one day found the pots and became rich. After that Faustino never came out again. What he probably did was come out to watch over his pots. It seems those Spaniards were friends of his, and he wanted to leave them that money. They left lots of coins scattered all around and people rushed to gather them up. The Spaniards ran away. If they hadn't, they would have had to give fifty percent to the government. Since Faustino didn't come out again, people forgot about him, but I have a good memory of what he was like. What I don't do is think much about it because it's exhausting.

Thinking tires you out. Nowadays, there are people who don't believe the dead reappear, or any of that, because they haven't seen it. Anyway, they're tired out just the same. They think about modern things, about the peoples of the world, about wars, and all the rest. They spend their time on that, and they get any recreation. Others set about to wallow around in vices and cheating. Life passes by between the vices and trying to find a way to start thinking. Even though you tell them about it, they don't pay attention. And they don't believe. Or hear.

I told the story of the little devil once to a youngster, and he told me that it was a lie. But it's true even though it seems like a lie. A man can create a little devil. Yessir, a little devil.

An old Congo from the Timbirito sugarmill was the one who taught me how to make it. He spent hours talking to me. He did nothing but tell me that I had to learn to work the stick-magic because I was serious and reserved. You should have heard him tell stories. He had seen everything. What was down here below, and what was up above, too. To tell the truth, he was a little crotchety, but I understood him. I never told him, "You don't know what you're talking about." I didn't laugh at him. That old timer was like a father to me. But anyway, back to the little devil. He showed me how to make him. One day when I was passing by, he sat me down in a place alone, looked at me, and started to say to me, "Criollo, come along to where I tell you. I will give to you a present of one thing." I figured it was money or some amulet, but nothing of the kind. He went on with his long sort of tangled-up story, "Criollo, you is a fool," and he showed me a vial he took out of his pocket. "Look, you see this, with this you get everything." That was when I realized the thing he was talking about was witchcraft. I learned to make the little devil, to raise him, and all. To do that you have to have more heart than anything else. A heart as cold as a fish. It isn't hard. You take a chicken egg with a spot. It has to have a spot in it because without it, it wouldn't work. Put it in the sun for two or three days. After it's hot, you put it in your armpit three Fridays in a row, and on the third Friday a little devil is hatched instead of a little chick. A little devil the color of a chameleon. Now, that little devil is put into a tiny, clear vial so you can see inside, and you sprinkle in some dried wine. Next, you keep it in your pant's pocket, good and secure so it won't escape, because those little devils tend to be scrappy. They move around a lot by wiggling their tail.

That's how you get what you want. Of course you can't ask for everything all at once. The idea is little by little. There comes a time of the year when you have to get rid of the little devil because you have been around with him quite a bit. So, you take it to the river at night and throw it in so the current will drag it off. It's true, the witch who carries one of those can't cross that river again. If he goes by there twenty times, the evil curse falls on him twenty times over.

It's good to do those tasks on Tuesdays. At least I've heard it said that way. When a witch wanted to work evil stick-magic, he chose Tuesdays. Tuesdays are the devil's days, that's why they are so evil. It seems that the devil had to choose a day, and he decided on that one. To tell the truth each time I hear that word, Tuesday, just that, Tuesday, I go prickly inside. I feel the devil in person. If they were going to prepare a mean cazuela de mayombe, they did it on Tuesday. It had more power that way. It was made with beef, bones of Christians, shin bones mainly. Shin bones are good for the evil curse. Then it was taken to an ant hill and was buried there. On Tuesdays always.

It was left in the ant hill for two or three weeks. One day, also a Tuesday, it had to be dug up. That was when they swore an oath that meant saying to the prenda, "I will do evil and do your bidding." That oath was spoken at twelve o'clock midnight, which is the devil's hour, and what the Congo swore became a contract with the devil. In a pact with the Congo devil. The oath was no joke or a tall tale. It had to be done right. If not, a person could even die all of sudden.

There are a lot of people who die like that, without sickness. It's a punishment from the devil. After the oath is spoken, and the prenda dug up, it was taken to the house, placed in a corner, and other ingredients were put in it to nourish it. The offerings were Guinea pepper, garlic, and guaguao peppers, a dead man's skull, and a shin bone wrapped in a black cloth. That cloth wrapping was placed over the cazuela, and...take care, whoever happened to look in there! The cazuela, when it first came into the house didn't work, but when all those offerings were put into it, the devil himself would be frightened. There was no spell it couldn't work. It's also true that the cazuela had its lightning stone and its vulture stone, which were nothing less than evil.

I seen just about every kind of terrible hex done with that. It killed people, derailed trains, burned houses down, well...When you hear talk of black magic you have to stay calm and be respectful. Respect is what opens doors to everything. That was how I learned about things.

That Congo man from Timbirito told me a great deal about his encounters with the devil. He saw the devil every time he wanted to. I think the devil is an opportunist. To bring harm and to give himself pleasure, he comes when you call him. But don't call him to do good, shit no! If anyone wanted to make a pact with him, they should take a hammer and a big spike. The old man told me. A hammer and a big spike. You look for a young ceiba tree out in the open, and you give the trunk three good blows with hammer so he hears them. As soon as the bastard hears that call, he comes real calm and sassy, he comes like someone who doesn't want a damn thing. Sometimes he dresses up like people. He never shows up as the devil. It doesn't suit him to scare you because he's strange and fearsome naturally—all red like a lick of fire, with his mouth full of flames, and a lance in the shape of a pitch fork in his hand. When he appears, you can speak to him normally. You do have to have very clear about what you say to him because for him years are just days, and if you promise him you're going to do something in three years, he understands three days. If you don't know that trick, you're screwed. I knew it from slavery times on. The devil reckons different from man. He uses another process. No one gives himself over to wickedness more than him. I don't know how he is now, but before he used to grease the wheels for everything. He made sure that things got done.

Anyone could summon him. Many people from the aristocracy called him. Counts and Marquises. Those same ones who said they were Christians and Masons. They never have convinced me with that business of the Masons. Where there's a secret, there's witchcraft, and there's no one more secret than a Mason. I have no doubts they have the devil in their religion. Although the thing with the devil of the Congos they learned from the elders themselves. The elders taught the Counts and Marquises to work stick-magic and they said to them, "While you work mayombe, you'll be lords of the earth." The Counts obeyed everything the elders ordered them to do. They took dirt from the four winds, wrapped it in corn husks, and made four little piles, each with a chicken foot tied to it, and carried it all to the cazuela so the request would be fulfilled. If there was anything wrong, they struck the cazuela with feverfew, and then, as they say, get going. Those cazuelas built up tremendous power. They could turn against anyone and denounce them.

The Congos used many types of charms. Any little stick or bone could be a good charm. I used some while at the Ariosa. In the war, too. I carried one that helped me a lot. I was never killed, thanks to it. I was wounded once, but it was in my thigh, and it was healed with camphor.

The best charms are made with little stones. All you had to do was fill up a soft little leather pouch and wear it around your neck. What you can't do is abandon it. You have to feed it frequently, just like people. The food is selected by the owner of the prenda, who is the one who makes the charm. They are almost always fed with garlic and guaguao pepper. Also, they are given rum to drink, and a pinch of Guinea pepper is sprinkled on them. The day one of those black witches delivered a charm, he looked at you real good and clapped your hands together, squeezed them hard, and held them together for a time. First, you told him that you weren't going to do anything bad with it and that while you were wearing it, you would have nothing to do with sex.

A magic charm is a delicate thing. The man who goes to bed with a woman while he's wearing a charm is making a mistake. His path will certainly be crooked for a long time. Besides, women make your magic weaker. After you do your thing with them, if you want to put on your charm, you have to scrub your hands with ashes to pacify and scare the evil away. If not, the charm itself will rebel against you.

Women weaken everything, from charms to cazuelas. That's why they have their special forms of magic. They can be witches but they can't work men's cazuelas. There are some who are more powerful than men, fiercer. I think they work better at cleansings and refreshenings. No one better than women for cleansing and freshening

I don't remember the woman who taught me about kerosene cans but I know it was years ago. It's the best thing for refreshening. You just take a big can and fill it with herbs and water. You can get those herbs in rich people's gardens. You mix them all up, basil, apasote, pine nuts, put them in the can with a little sugar and salt. You take the can out to a corner of the house, and after two days you sprinkle the water inside in all the corners. The water may smell, but it refreshes. After a short time you feel a soft breeze that comes in through the doors. It's the healthiest thing there is. Also, if you want, you can take a bath with it by leaving out the salt and the sugar.

The bath should be taken at noon with the sun straight overhead. Seven baths are sufficient for a good cleansing. In the past, people took those baths daily. The Congos used them for their health. They were also called Congo hexes, witchcraft, though people said it was spiritualism.

Spirits are weaker than witchcraft. I didn't pay much attention to what the old people said to me. I just went along with it a little so as not to upset them. Men like me aren't very partial to witchcraft because we don't have the patience. I liked mischief and joking around a lot, and you can't practice witchcraft that way. I like to see and hear for myself to keep from being fooled. What bothered me was that I was told that such and such a thing couldn't be touched or known about. So, I would get angry and want to have my own way.

Once I did a bad thing that gives me the creeps every time I remember it. The creeps! I go to the house of a santero, and I begin to look through the rooms, the closets, the cupboards, everything. The santero sees me, and doesn't say anything. But the I decide to go to the end room, where the drums and the white cloths and the soup tureens and the saints are. I go in there, and I begin to have myself a banquet on the bananas, sweets, and coconut. When I come out pretty stuffed, I bump into the santero, and he looks at me and asks me, "What is going on?" I don't say a thing to him, and he keeps going. But I think that contact itself makes my legs begin to shake, and they tremble and tremble like I was sick. Well, I had to leave. Truth is that the

trembling was for no reason because the santero didn't catch
me. If he had, then yes. The food that's put out for the
saints shouldn't be touched. But when hunger calls, a person
isn't his own master. The Congos wouldn't have done that
even in jest. A Congo would see you sticking your snout in
the wrong places and watch out! They could even do you
harm. The Congos have more power than the Lucumí. They
are harder headed. They work magic with material objects.
It's all based on sticks, bones, blood, trees in the forest...

For the Congos a tree is a very important thing. From it
everything is born, and in it everything is given. It's like a
god. You feed it, it talks, it asks for things, you take care of it.
The Congos get everything from nature, from the tree,
which is the soul of nature. Witchcraft has to seek help from
the trees and the herbs. All of the sugarmills during slavery
had their groves and good trees. On account of that, the
place was hopeful for the Congos. At the Ariosa there were
large cultivated plots and overgrown places, too. In those
forests there used to be and still is witchcraft. You can see
spirits and lights appear, and all kinds of other things
parading by, but then, as time has passed, it's faded from my
memory. Things that you can't put into words, things whose
natures are not known to us, or what forms they take.
Mysteries, shall we say. The most amazing thing I've seen
were the old Congos who turned into animals, beasts. That
was a hell of a thing.

They were so evil it made your hair stand on end and
gave you goose bumps. Sometimes they said that so and so,
the palero, had left the batey as a cat or a dog. Or, if not that,
some black woman would come running out yanking at her
hair shouting, "Ay, help, I saw a dog the size of my
husband!" That dog could be the husband in person, in the
person of a dog, I mean.

I think I never seen these things, but even just the stories are scary enough, and in those years people spent their time making up stories. To think that a dog with rabies could be a wicked old Congo son of a bitch would make anyone's hair stand on end. Later on, those things were never seen again in Cuba. At least no one has come out with a similar story. At times I think that it all happened because there were many Africans here. Today, there are no Africans in Cuba, and the new people don't give a hoot about religion. They think life is nothing but eating, sleeping, and lots of dough. That's why we're like we are. Wars here, wars there. You have to have a faith. Believe in something. If not, we're all screwed.

If you don't believe in miracles today, you will tomorrow. There are proofs of it everyday. Some stronger than others but all convincing. There are moments when you feel very confident, and you let go of the reins. Disillusionment sets in. At such times, there are no saints, no miracles. But those times pass quickly. Man lives and thinks in serenity.

When you feel sort of hot inside, swollen, stuck, so you can't move your jaw, that's when you're not thinking, and if you do, you tend to be thinking bad thoughts. That's when danger is born. In those moments. To relieve that situation you have to have cool water around. Two or three weeks are enough to refresh the atmosphere. Cool water is very good. I think it decongests the brain. It rises without evaporating. If a lot of water does get used up, the glass has to be refilled. That means it's doing its job. In the barracoons, everybody had his little glass of water and his herbs hanging from the wall. They were no fools. I never seen the owners' houses inside, but for sure they had theirs, too. They were pretty strong believers.

Catholicism always falls into spiritism. That has to be taken for granted. There is no such thing as a one-hundred percent pure Catholic. The rich from back then were Catholics, but they paid heed to witchcraft once in awhile.

Not to speak of the overseers. They had their eye on the black witches out of the fear they had for them. They well, knew that if the witches wanted to, they could crack you open like a beetle. Even today many people say to you "I'm an Apostolic Catholic." What! Tell that story to someone else. Hereabouts, the biggest and the littlest has his small missal, his regla book. No one is so pure as all that. All the religions have become mixed up together in this country. The African brought his, the strongest, and the Spaniard also brought his, though not so strong. They all have to be respected. That's my way of doing things.

The African religions are more entertaining. You dance, sing, enjoy yourself, fight. There is maní, palo, quimbumbia. When the sun went down, groups would begin to form. Quimbumbia and brujo were the same. They almost always used drums. The same drums for playing palo. Quimbumbia was a Congo game. At one time around here, the two groups of black witches used to divide up to have a competition. They carefully planted a bunch of banana trees in the center of a circle drawn on the ground. Then, each witch went about casting spells on the trees so they would bear fruit. They went around in front of them and kneeled down, gargled mouthfuls of rum at them three or four times, and the one who made the trees bear fruit won the contest right then. The winner ate the fruit, and if he wanted to, he shared it with his people.

After a while, to celebrate, they played the drums and danced. The winner was called King Rooster, and they shoved him out to dance. Each time those groups went to play quimbumbia they looked for a handful of sticks to strengthen themselves. If you ask me that quimbumbia wasn't so cruel. There was another that certainly was. It was done by skinning a live rooster and then killing him. All the feathers and the guts were put in a big pot to cook. Once the rooster was cooked, you started to eat him, and the bones that remained were thrown into the pot. Rooster bones are the strongest kind for magic.

That rooster, all eaten up like he was, would tease any Christian because after you had swallowed him, he jumped out of the pot when people least expected it. He would appear in middle of the uproar and the squeaking of the leather stools. It seemed as though he was whole, and he was.

That game of quimbumbia was almost always played at night. Of course in those days there was no electricity, and the mills were lit with kerosene lanterns made of tin. Those lanterns were used to make light for Quimbumbia, though for witchcraft the dark is good. The spirits won't come down in the light. They are like the albinos who only see in the dark.

Electricity came first to Santa Clara. Right into the city. The philanthropist Marta Abreu brought it. It didn't come to the Ariosa until...well, I don't remember, but it was after the Caracas mill. Caracas brought in electric light in that area of Lajas. In the biggest mill in Cuba. The owners were millionaires, and that was why they bought the electricity. Their name was Terry. I don't really know where I was, up in a tree or on top of a roof. But I saw the lights of the Caracas mill, which were a marvel.

I used kerosene lanterns for light in the barracoon. You could buy them at the storekeeper's. I imagine the other owners were jealous of the lights and all that luxury at the Caracas. It's just that the Terrys were aristocrats, very refined. They went to France every year. The oldest of them was don Tomás Terry. I seen him a lot from a distance. He was a man ahead of the times with the ideas he had. Emilio, his son, was like that, too. But don Tomás was better. All the workers loved him, and to his credit he made friends with the black Congos. He helped them a good deal. He even got to the point of giving them money so the Congos could establish their cabildos. He treated them well. People said he enjoyed himself with the blacks, watching them dance. In Cruces there was a Congo cabildo, founded by don Tomás, and another in Lajas. I seen the two of them, and I was in them. I went to look for women. There were beautiful black women there! But if you got the least bit crude, you were tossed out on your ear. Those black women knew how to put a man in his place.

I recall that in the cabildo at Cruces there was a photograph of don Tomás Terry. I wish all slave owners had been like him and his sons. I don't know anything about them nowadays. They must be in France, strolling around and living like the millionaires they are.

At Ariosa it was different. It wasn't miserable at all, but it didn't have the luxury or the style of the Caracas. The boiler house was lit with big gas lanterns, and the batey too in harvest time because in the fallow season it was as dark as a wolf's stomach. At the entrance to the barracoon they always left a little light on. That was all. That was why the men got bored and thought only about women. That was my obsession, and still is. I still think that women are the most important thing in life. When I got a woman under my skin, you should have seen me. I was the devil himself. Bashful, but ready. The women of Remedios were famous for their beauty. To see them, it was best to go to the fiestas that were given there every year. I think I went to at least ten of those fiestas. There I seen lots of women! They were religious fiestas, and fun. Both things. More religious, but...

All fiestas have their entertainments. If not, they aren't fiestas. Remedios was a serious place, though, because of religion. It was always a very religious town and very serious. All the houses had altars with male and female saints. Some ugly, others pretty. People from Remedios were well known for having good fiestas during Holy Week. They were dressed in black through almost the entire week, very solemn, and silent. They didn't allow anyone to come into town on horseback, much less wearing spurs. Those were days to stay inside. Trains couldn't blow a whistle. It had the silence of a cemetery. On Maundy Thursday you couldn't sweep the house because the whites said it was the same as sweeping the head of God. You couldn't wash with water because the water would turn to blood. You wouldn't believe it! They didn't kill birds or pigs. It was the white man's mourning, and they said that whoever ate was a sinner and deserved to be punished. But I seen lots of campesinos put away a suckling pig during those days.

There were many strange customs in Remedios, most of all during the days of Holy Week. I know about them pretty much because I liked that town and went there often. The Ariosa was right next to it. I remember a custom that made cousins who were going to get married pay a dispensation to God. Marriage between cousins was looked down upon, and that's why they had to pay, in order to not fall into sin. Of course that arrangement was good for the priests. Right there they had another hand out. It's also true that the business of marrying among cousins is ugly, but when a woman gets into a man's fancy, there's no God who can control him.

One thing that was done in secret on those days was to play dominoes or cards. On Holy Saturday, when Lent was ended, people played in the doorways. The rest of the days they had to keep hidden. Bowling was so strictly prohibited that it wasn't even played in secret. In Remedios there were two or three unused bowling places. There were raffles with cards. Two cards were purchased. Whoever bought them signed his name or put his mark on the back. The same person who dealt the cards collected the money. Then he picked up a knife, and turned the card. If the seven came up, he won the raffle. It's a mystery about the number seven. It's like the number three, and eight, which is death. You could play better in silence and in secret. It was more interesting. The rich whites didn't play any of this during Holy Week. They said there had to be total grief for the disappearance of Christ. To my mind, they deceived people. I know Christ is the son of God, that he came from nature. But this thing about his dying is still unclear. The truth is that I've seen him many a time, but I didn't know who it was.

In all the mills, work went on during Holy Week. Except for Monday, Tuesday, and Holy Saturday, after ten o'clock in the morning, when Christ was raised up. The owners waited for Christ to rise up in order to take advantage of you again. There were those who after Resurrection began to do some witchcraft. The fiesta began at that hour in Remedios. Holy Saturday was the most fun day of the whole year. A Judas was burned like in the fiesta of San Juan. The Judas was a big fat dummy that was hung from a rope and hit with sticks. Then it was burned to a crisp until there was nothing left as a reminder of his betrayal of Jesus. The Judas was the enemy of Christians, the one who had assassinated Christ, as the whites said. He killed Christ in a war of Jews. They told me all of that once, but some of it has slipped away over the years. What I do know is that he existed and that he was Christ's assassin. That's for certain.

I haven't seen a town more partial to old customs than Remedios. Everything there was done out of passion, and watch out not go along with them. During the fiestas, all the people of Remedios had a duty to go and have fun, and during Holy Week, whoever didn't walk around being religious was understood to be a traitor. Or they said he had Satan behind him. Naturally, that was among the whites because they had nothing to say to the campesinos. They went to church and to the fiestas because of whatever religious feeling they had. Parents made their children pray and sing in the mass that was held in the streets. You saw those important men singing, and it made you laugh how bad they did it. They strolled along the streets dressed in black, holding candles and little books in their hands. On their heads, the rich women wore some big things that looked like a comb that opened up and had little holes. They looked pretty.

Back then, children couldn't make their own decisions. At twenty five they could decide some things. The parents had them under their control. That was why they all went to church and prayed. It happened that way in town just the same as in the countryside.

There was a fellow there who was no great friend of the church. His name was Juan Celorio. He got together the little children every time there was a feast day, and on Sundays too, to entertain himself. He was an Asturian and the owner of a big store. As the children were passing by, to attract them he would give them sweets, coffee with milk, bread, and butter, and all they asked for. He talked to them a lot. He told them that instead of going to church, they should have a good time. The parents were furious with him, and they didn't want to see hide nor hair of him. Celorio was a good man. The little ones, each time they could get out, would go to see him to get something to eat. Then Celorio gave them cans, sheets of steel, picks, iron railings, and ox horns. Horns that were sharp on one end and filled with wax at the wide end. They were decorated with turkey feathers, and they made a sound from the same end. The noise was deafening. So, with those noises and those cans, Celorio organized processions through the town. Many people joined in with them. The biggest and the littlest were looking for a good time. That's how the famous carousings got started.

I seen other things in Remedios those Holy Saturdays. That town was like an inferno. It was absolutely packed. You could as easily run into a rich man as into a poor one, and everybody out in the streets. The corners were swarming with people.

The town became festive, full of fire works, lanterns, serpentines...The puppeteers would arrive, and they began to dance and do acrobatics. I remember them perfectly. There were gypsies, Spaniards, and Cubans. The Cubans were very bad. They didn't have the gypsies' humor or their strangeness. There were performances in the parks and halls. In the parks it was very hard to see what was going on because the people formed a ring around them and blocked them completely. They sang and screamed. The children were crazy happy with the big puppets that walked and were moved by strings. There were also actors who would dress up like clowns with suits made of big panels of colors or with stripes and hats. They jumped around, gave out hard candy, and ate anything people would give them, and they got down on the ground so a big stone could be put on their stomach that a person from the audience would split in two with a sledge hammer. The clown would stand up quickly and bow. Every one thought he had left his ribs pounded into the ground, but not a bit of it. They knew how to bring off the trick. They had been doing their tricks for so many years that not one of them went wrong.

They performed everything that had been and was to be. They earned their living that way. They were fun and got along with everyone. A clown would eat burning paper, and after a bit he would pull colored ribbons out of his mouth. The flames turned into ribbons. People gasped with surprise because there was no way of explaining it.

The gypsies were the best. They were comical and serious. When their performances were over, they were serious and didn't enjoy being friendly. They wore the loudest colored clothes. The men were a little dirty. They wore vests and kerchiefs tied around their heads, covering up their foreheads. Red kerchiefs mostly. The women dressed in wide, colorful skirts. They wore bracelets on their arms and covered their fingers with rings. They kept their hair black as jet, well groomed, and down to their waist. It had a natural shine. The gypsies came from their own country, and truth is that I don't remember what country, but it was far away. They did speak Spanish. They had no houses. They lived in a clump of tents. They made their tents with four poles and a thick canvas. So they slept on the ground wherever they pleased.

In Remedios they camped in empty lots or on the porches of abandoned houses. They only stayed a few days. All they did was go to the fiestas. Their lives were like that, running around and drinking. When they liked a place and wanted to stay, they brought the whole gang, including the children and animals. Sometimes the government police had to come and throw them out. But they didn't put up a fuss; they just loaded up their poles and boxes and looked for someplace new.

They didn't even worry about food; they just cooked on the ground. They always seemed nice to me. Like witches, they could tell fortunes. They did it with cards. The women went out to work fortune-telling and almost forced people listen to them. And they were convincing because they knew a great deal from traveling around so much. The gypsies had monkeys, little dogs, and birds. They taught the monkeys to dance and to hold out their hands for coins. They were skinny monkeys, not well fed. The little dogs danced, too, and stood on their hind feet.

I think there are still gypsies like that in Cuba. Since they move around a lot, maybe they're lost out there, scattered in among the little towns.

Another pastime during Holy Week were the raffles. On Holy Saturday, of course. They raffled off scarves, colognes, rose pomades, and sewing machines. Cheap scarves and stinky colognes. I never used cologne because I didn't want to get chilled. There are people who don't have the constitution for it. Nobody won the sewing machines. They were bait for the suckers. People bought a lot of tickets, but I never seen anybody walk away with a machine. And they spent hours at the counters waiting for that sewing machine. I got really angry to see how people spent everything and no sewing machine. If it had been up to me, I would have put an end to those raffles. Above all for the poor souls who went around afterward in the streets with their hands cupped, begging for water.

That happened in Holy Week, and the religious people themselves encouraged it. Even today raffles are a monstrous fraud. And even more so among the priests. More than ten years ago I went to a church close to Arroyo Apolo, where there are lots of papaya groves, with a whole parade of veterans. The priests had invited us. One of them, the one who said mass, tried to interest the vets with words of Christ and other foolishness. He even said that the communists had to be exterminated and that they were the sons of the devil. I got really pissed off because in those years I was affiliated with the Popular Socialist Party on account of the organization it had and its ideas. Mostly for the ideas, which were for the welfare of the workers. I never went back to that church again. And I never seen the priest again, either. But I did find out from an old gossip, who got in as a friend of mine, that the priest had given a fiesta in the church's patio and that he had put on a big raffle. He raffled things, and all the vets got little scarves, little socks, and a bunch of junk. I realized that it was the same trick as before and that raffles continued to be tricks. That's why I don't believe in any of them.

At the Holy Saturday fiestas they had variety shows. They don't exist anymore, but back then they held them at all the fiestas. They were fun because you would see the strangest things in the world in them. They set it all up with some old poles and a canvas with decorations. Many times without the decorations. Some comics would come up and begin to goof around. They would act like monkeys for the audience. They sang ditties, made up stories, jokes, pranks, predictions. Whatever occurred to them. It was another trick to collect money. When they were held in a hall, people had to pay to get in. Both blacks and whites would go.

Cubans have always liked having variety shows in the theaters. In Havana I went to a theater once, and it seemed to me I seen vaudeville. It was a comedy between a black man and a white man. No, for me that was playing the monkey. No matter how they dressed him up...

Remedios was a town of old-time habits. They did the oldest things in the world there. On the days of Corpus Christi, it really caught your eye to see how the blacks would come out of the cabildos dressed as little devils with bright red daubed on their clothes, hoods that covered their heads, and bells around their waists. Those little devils were like scarecrows for the children. They came out of the Congo cabildos. They weren't ñáñigos because there was no ñáñigo movement in Remedios. They were the Congos' little devils.

The blacks of Remedios had two social clubs, one for recreation, around the corner from Brigadier González street, and one for religious affairs. They would gather together in both of them. In the one for recreation, an orchestra made up entirely of blacks rehearsed for Holy Week. That orchestra played danzones and danzas. In the old days, the danza was very popular. The blacks danced it in the street and in the halls.

The orchestra didn't always play for blacks. Sometimes it would go to the "Tertulia," a club for whites, and made pleasant sounds around there for awhile. The musicians got good pay. I never danced to a band. My pleasure was women. As soon as I got to town I began to sniff around and brought out my net. I always managed to make a good catch.

The people of Remedios, like people in other towns in that area, had breakfast early. Around six thirty or seven the table was served. Poor people's breakfast was even earlier, and if they were from outside of town, even more so. Poor people had coffee and sweet potato. The tastiest kind of sweet potato cooked over the ashes, the African way. Lunch was between eleven and eleven-thirty. In well-to-do houses, there was no shortage of bread, butter, or wine. They didn't have the habit of drinking water. It was all wine, wine, wine. Dinner was at eight-thirty or nine. It was the biggest meal of the day. People in town went to bed at midnight. But in the countryside, at eight or nine everyone was already worn out. Dandies could get up at ten in the morning. Now, a campesino who had to break his back working on the land to eat, he got up at five in the morning at the latest. People drank a lot of coffee. Every household had an abundance of big, black, iron coffee pots where they made coffee. They roasted it in the house themselves. If you didn't have a grinder, you had a mortar and pestle. Hand-ground coffee is the kind I like the best because it keeps its aroma. That's probably just an idea of mine, but an idea is an idea. Before coffee plantations got bigger, coffee was sold in the pharmacy. After that, by peddlers in the street. Coffee became big business. I knew people who did only that business. They sold unroasted coffee.

Around Remedios, agualoja was very popular. The agualojeros sold it on the street. It was made from water, sugar, honey and cinnamon. It tasted heavenly. I used to give myself whole bellyfuls. The old Lucumí women made one that was really delicious. They didn't skimp on anything. The Congo women made it, too.

Anytime an African did something, he did it well. He brought the recipe from his land, from Africa. Of the things I liked the most, the best were the fritters that you don't see around anymore because of laziness. Because of people just sitting around and doing sloppy work. These days, people don't have the gusto to make those things. They make food without salt or lard, and it isn't worth a mustard seed. But back then, you should have seen the care taken, above all by the old black women, to make chucherías. Those crispy fried things were sold on the street on wooden tables or on big platters that they carried in a basket on their heads. You would call to a Lucumí woman and say to her: "Ma Petrona, Ma Dominga, come on over here." She would come over all dressed up in white linen or cotton, shiney clean, and answer, "Half a peso, my child." You gave her a half peso or two and started right in eating little fritters of yuca, black eyed peas, taro, or doughnuts...and twenty more things. They called all those foods granjerías. On feast days more street vendors were out than on other days. But if you wanted to eat chucherías, there was always an old woman on a corner with her portable stove ready.

Punch was sold on the street as well as in the store. More likely on the street on feast days. I will never forget that kind of punch. It had no oranges or rum or anything like that. It was made from pure egg yolks, sugar and alcohol. That was all. It was made by putting all the ingredients in a clay bowl or in a big tin can and beating it with a wooden stirrer in the shape of a pineapple that you spun between your hands. You mixed it good and drank it. You couldn't put the egg whites in because they would cut it. They sold it for a half peso a glass. Good and cheap. Punch was very common at baptisms. Among the Africans it was never absent. They drank it to be happy, though truth to tell, in the old days baptisms were happy occasions on their own. They would turn into fiestas.

The Africans were in the habit of baptizing their children forty days after birth. So to prepare for that day they would gather more and more half pesos. All the children had godparents. And the godparents were supposed to bring half pesos to the baptism. They changed gold coins, doubloons and other coins for half pesos. They would make little green and scarlet colored ribbons and tie the half pesos up through a small hole in the middle. Girls were supposed to string those ribbons. The day of the baptism the godparents would come smiling with their pockets full of half pesos—their pockets sticking out like oars on a rowboat. After the baptism and the big meal, they would go into the patio, and there they would call the children who would come running like the wind. When they were all gathered around, the godparents would throw the half pesos in the air, and the little beggars would go crazy trying to catch them. That was another curious thing from those times. In Remedios, it never failed to happen. That's where the phrase "Godfather, a half peso" comes from. I was a godfather two times, but I can't remember my godchildren. Everything gets mixed up in life, and sometimes people remember other people, and others don't. That's the way it is. You can't do anything about it. Ingratitude goes on and on.

The most beautiful thing in the world is to see men joined in brotherhood. You see more of that in the country than in the city. In the city, in all the towns, there are a lot of bad people—the kind of rich people who believes they own the world and don't help anyone. In the country it's different. There, all the people have to live together, like in a family. There has to be happiness.

I remember that in that whole district of Las Villas people helped each other a great deal. Neighbors were like family. If someone needed something because they wanted to move or plant something or bury some relative, they had help right away. Houses made of palm, for example, can be raised in two days. And that was possible on account of people gathered in a work gang to help do the job. They would put a roof on a person's house in a few hours. Or, if not that, they would help him plow. Each neighbor brought his yoke of oxen. They broke the earth, first in a single furrow, then crisscrossed. They did it that way so it would be fertile. That operation was called crossing the land. The same for during planting it. They all did it together so the poor man wouldn't get exhausted and quit. They knew that a man couldn't do it all by himself in the beginning. The tenant farmers would give the new neighbor some of their seeds. After he sowed the seed, he had to weed the field. So everyone pitched in with the hoeing around the plants so that the soil would be loose and fertile. Packed dirt doesn't bring a crop. It has to be good and loosened up.

All of that was done as a sign of friendship. There was one little trick, a practical joke that was a bit mean perhaps, but people enjoyed it. A campesino took to eyeing the pigs of another campesino. When that kind of thing happened, a person put his mark on his pigs' ears. If a campesino happened to make off with a pig that wasn't his, he slaughtered it and gave a fiesta where he invited all his friends. They all got together, and the roasted pig was put on a cedar serving board on a table with his mouth full of wild flowers. The head with the marked ear was put out in plain sight, and that was when the real owner realized the big joke they were playing on him because they were all eating up his property. That was the funny part. Funny, so he didn't get angry. The happiest one there was supposed to be the animal's owner.

I see all that as a proof of friendship. Today, people don't act that way. There's envy and jealousy everywhere. That's why I like the solitary life. I don't mess with anybody and they don't mess with me. I didn't even go around in groups in the old days. I always went around alone. Once in a while when an unattached woman followed me, I would let her. But the thing about sticking together with people for life doesn't work with me. As old as I am, I have no enemies, and the ones I do have won't even speak to me so as to avoid trouble.

In Remedios I knew lots of people. I spent all my time around there in the 90s. I would go from the Ariosa to town in the time it takes to say "Amen." I know the customs, and I know what people are like. I know how they think when they look at you. Rich people were the least worried about gossip. They spent their lives with their music and dances. And with their money, of course.

The women of the town played the harp in the front rooms with the windows open so everyone would see them. Later came the piano. But first it was the harp. It didn't attract my attention. And peeping inside a house always seemed so impolite to me, though that was the custom. I preferred drums and danzas. The danzas of the ordinary folks' band. But since for the blacks the harp was new, they stood in front of the window and stared and stared. The fact is that all those families, the Rojas, the Manuelillos, the Carrillos, they all lived in their own world. Business, fiestas, money. They didn't care anything about gossip. Poor people yes, because they lived closer together, and more...The rich are rich, and the poor are poor.

That was everything I seen in Remedios. Many blacks didn't go to the fiestas because they were old or bound to tribal ways. I allowed myself a few turns on account of the young ladies. What beauties! Then, I would take to my road at night with my machete in my belt so that no one would jump me. If it hadn't rained, I would get to the mill real quick. If I got tired on the trip, I lay down to sleep in the cane until my legs would let me continue on my way. The cane is cool in the early morning.

The next day I would set to telling stories. I would get together with some old men, and I would tell them stories. I preferred the old timers to the youngsters. I always liked them better. I still prefer them. Maybe because I'm old now...but no, before, as a young man, I thought the same. They listened to my stories. What I used to tell them about the fiestas, about Judas, about the drinks and the games. They asked me if there was respect and seriousness. I was embarrassed to tell them some of the filthy details, and I kept quiet. Of course, I still felt bad. How could you tell one of those old folks that a person was capable of lying down with a black woman in the bushes? Just like they listened to you, you had to listen to them. Pay attention to them with your eyes and with your ears. They were sincere about everything. They would say to you very calmly, "Child, you don' hear, you don' notice nothin', you get on the way home, git!" You had to take off like a shooting star. Even though they were short on talk, they liked you to listen to them when they spoke. They talked about the land, about Africa, about animals and ghosts. They didn't go around gossiping or joking. Anyone who told them a lie got punished severely. To get along with those old men you had to be quiet and respectful. A boy joked around once with an old man, and the old timer said to him, "Listen, just as the sun be goin' down, so you best be goin' on." And so it was because the system was the same as during slavery: you take the dirt from the boy's footsteps and toss it in a cazuela until sunset. That was how the old folks got rid of the jokesters. The thing is that the old ones were amazing. They knew where the gnat laid her eggs. You would go up to them, and they could solve everything, with money or without it. But when you asked them something, they said, "You go, do this magic, and when you solve your problem, you come back to me, and pay me." You had to obey those words. Before the consultation you always had to pay twenty-five centavos. That was separate from the other payment which was bigger. Whoever didn't make the bigger payment, which was secret, was in bad trouble. He would get stabbed within a few days, he would lose his wife, or they fired him at work...something always happened. You couldn't play around with an old man from Africa. Even today, a young palero is not so demanding. Anyway, an old black man has another way of doing things. He's more serious, more straightforward, more...

The old men loved to tell stories. Stories and gossip. They made up stories at all hours, noon and night. They always had the urge to tell about things. There were so many stories that most of the time you couldn't keep track of them, they made you so dizzy. I pretended to be listening, but the truth was that in the end it all got scrambled up in my head. In the barracoons of the Ariosa there were two or three blacks from the old country of Africa. I think that an old bow-legged woman who was there was Arará. I'm not sure. The others were Congos. There was a difference between the Africans and the criollos. The Africans understood each other. The criollos almost never understood the Africans well. They would listen to them, but they didn't understand them clearly. I could communicate with them because I spent my whole life listening to them. They liked me a lot.

Even today I remember Ma Lucía. I first met her off the Ariosa. I don't know if it was in Remedios or Zulueta, but in any case I seen a lot of her later on in Santa Clara. I used to go there to parties. I got along with her very well. She was a dark black woman, rather tall, and Lucumí. She devoted herself to santería all the while I knew her. She had a passel of godchildren, being so well-known. Ma Lucía was a story teller. She spent a good deal of time fussing with her clothes, her white dress, her cotton blouse, out of vanity. She wore a hairdo you don't see today, piled up. She said it was African. She made sweets and amalá. She sold them on the street and in the bateyes of the mills when people were getting off work to go running around town. She made a lot of money.

She managed to buy a house in Santa Clara after the war. She left that house to a daughter. One day she called me and said to me, "You is good and quiet. I going to be telling to you something." Then she started telling all sorts of African stories. But I can't remember hardly any of them. I confuse them and mix them up, and then I don't know if I'm talking about an elephant or a tortoise. That's because of age, although there are other things I remember well. But old age is old age, and it's not given to us for pleasure.

Thing is that Ma Lucía told me about some African customs I never seen hereabouts. Neither had she, and that's why she remembered them. She told me that in her country all the men ever did was cut down the forest, and the women had to glean the land and gather the harvest, and after that make the meals for the family, which was very large. She said her family was bigger than a plantation work force. I think that was because in Africa the women give birth year after year. I once seen a photograph of Africa, and all the black women had swollen bellies and tits hanging down. Fact is that in Cuba I don't recall seeing that spectacle. Anyway, in the barracoon it was just the opposite. Women dressed up with layers of cloth and covered their breasts. Well, so as not to lose track of Mamá Lucía's stories...The business with the elephant was very strange. When she used to see one of those circuses that go from town to town, the ones that have elephants and monkeys, she would say, "You, criollo does not know what lilifant be. Lilifant in my country is big, big as the palm tree." I was speechless. It sure did seem exaggerated to me because then she would say that the elephants from her country weighed twenty or twenty-five tons. We boys would burst out laughing, though hiding it from her. Lots of things were lies, but others were true. Well, as far as I was concerned, they were lies though others believed them to be true. Heaven help you trying to tell one of those old women she was mistaken!

I remember the story of the tortoise and the toad. She told it to me a hundred times. The tortoise and the toad had carried on a feud for many years. The toad had tricked the tortoise because he was afraid of her. He thought she was stronger than he was. He took a gourd cup of food, and put it out for the tortoise. He almost stuck it in her mouth. The tortoise, upon seeing the cup full of food, was pleased. She ate until she nearly gagged. She didn't even think that the toad had put out the food for a reason. She was very naive. If you're naive you'll often be deceived. Later, full and contented, she began to walk through the woods looking for the toad who was hiding in a cave. When the toad saw her he spoke to her from a distance, "Here I am, tortoise, look." She looked, and saw nothing. She got tired and went away. She came to a pile of straw and lay down to rest. The toad caught her sleeping, and he poisoned her by peeing on her. She was sleeping because she was so full. That's why he was able to catch her. The moral of the tale is that people shouldn't be greedy. You have to have doubts about everyone. Your enemy can give you food to trick you.

Ma Lucía kept on telling me about the toad. She was afraid of them because she said that they had a deadly poison in their veins, that they had venom for blood. The proof is that when a person hurts a toad, if they throw a rock at one or hit one with a stick, it gets revenge by following the tracks of the person and poisoning him in the mouth or in the nose. Most of all in the mouth because almost everyone sleeps with their mouth open.

About the tiger she told me it was a treacherous animal that jumped down out of trees to catch men by the neck and kill them. It caught women by the neck, too, and made them do dirty things, like the orangutans do. Although orangutans were worse. According to Ma Lucía, an orangutan could find women by their scent and catch them by surprise so they couldn't move. All monkeys are like that. It's as if they were men with tails but dumb.

A monkey can fall in love with a woman. There have been cases here in Cuba. I heard talk of two women from rich families who slept with monkeys. Two sisters. One of them was from Santa Clara. The other I can't recall, but she had offspring because I seen those monkeys like lords of the castle. I went there one day for some reason I can't remember, and I found a monkey sitting on a chair in the entryway. So everything the old folks say isn't a lie. What happened was that we hadn't seen those things, and we doubted them or laughed at them. Today, after so much time has gone by, I find myself thinking about all this again, and the truth is that I come to the conclusion that the African was wise in all things. There are some who say they were from the wilds, and that they behaved like animals. There is no lack of white men out there who say it. I think different because I knew them. They weren't the least bit like animals. They taught me many things though they didn't know how to read or write. Customs that are more important than information. To be educated, not to meddle

in other folks' problems, speak softly, be respectful, be
religious, be a hard worker...All of that the Africans taught
me. They said to me, "Water falls on the taro leaf, but it does
not get wet." That was so I wouldn't go around looking for
trouble. I should listen, and be aware in order to defend
myself, but I shouldn't talk too much. Whoever talks too
much gets tangled up. How many people get flies in their
mouths from having their tongues always wagging!

Luckily, I am quiet. I won't forget the old folks' words.
Heck no! And when I hear people talking about simpletons, I
start to laugh. Let's see who is a simpleton. They called them
bozales to call them something because they spoke according
to the language of their country. They talked different, that
was all. I never took them to be simpletons. On the contrary,
I respected them. A black Congo or Lucumí knew more
about medicine than a doctor. More than a Chinese doctor!
They even knew when a person was going to die. That word,
bozal was incorrect. You don't hear it now because little by
little the Africans have been dying off. If there's one around
he has to be twenty times older than me.

Each black had a different physique, lips, or nose. Some
were darker than others, more reddish like the Mandingas
or more orange colored, like the Musongos. You could tell
from a distance what nation they belonged to. The Congos,
for example, were short. There were cases of tall Congos, but
it was very rare. The real Congo was short and stocky. The
Congo women likewise. The Lucumís were of all sizes. Some
more or less like the Mandingas, who were the tallest. I can't
explain that strangeness. It's a mystery without doubt. How
can there be men taller than other men?! God knows.

The Lucumís were good workers, ready for any job.
They even fought well in the war. In Carlos Manuel's war.[16]

Even though they weren't trained to fight, they joined the columns and showed their mettle. Later, when the war was over, they were returned to work, to slavery. That was why they were cynical about the next war. But they fought anyway. I never seen a Lucumí backing down. I never heard them bragging like war heroes, either. Other African blacks were always saying that the war was foolishness and that it changed nothing. That was because it had been a failure. Yet most of them put their bodies on the line during the War for Independence. I know myself that war destroys men's trust, your brothers die at your side, and there's nothing you can do about it. Then the opportunists come and take the good jobs. But still you have to keep slicing away with your machete. To be a coward and hide in a corner is to lose your dignity forever. Those old men, with the memory of the other war still fresh, joined up with the Independence. They served well but without enthusiasm. They really had lost their enthusiasm. Not their strength or bravery but their enthusiasm, yes. Besides, who the hell knew what they were throwing themselves into!

It was a great undertaking but very murky. There was a lot of confusion with the new war. You heard rumors that Spain would lose, that Cuba would be free. The real truth is that whoever threw himself into it was playing the last card in his deck. That's why you can't criticize the old folks, saying they weren't brave. They were. More than that, they were more dependable than the criollos. Everyone knows there were criollo partisans. You wouldn't catch the old folks joining the guerrilleros. That's the best proof. They fought with Carlos Manuel and gave a lesson in patriotism. I won't say they knew why they were fighting. But they went. When things are bad, you can't be going this way and that way. What you have to do is to put your body on the line. The

Cuban in those years, in the 70s and 80s, wasn't prepared to fight. He had the fortitude inside, but his hands were empty. It was harder to find weapons than a needle in a haystack. Even so they took a piece of indigo wood and made a dagger. With that dagger they faced an enemy with firearms. Generally speaking the Congos made them. Whoever they stabbed was left as stiff as a board. In my opinion, those daggers had some witchcraft on the tip. The Spaniards used to see a black with one of those daggers, and they would take to their heels. They used muskets, too, in the Ten Years War.

During the War of Independence there were firearms. The fighting was on a more equal footing. That was why we won. There were muskets, snub-nosed .45s, short carbines and some rifles. The high caliber guns were almost never used because ammunition was scarce. The Winchester rifle was used a lot and the blunderbuss, which was the bandits' favorite weapon. The African blacks, as well as the criollos, learned to use those weapons, and they fought like the devil. They were better equipped in that war.

Whenever I see one of those blacks in my memory, I see him fighting. They didn't talk about what they were going into or why. They just fought. To defend their lives, of course. When someone asked them how they felt, they would say, "Cuba libre, Me's a liberator." Not a one wanted to continue under Spanish rule. You could put an official seal on that. Not a one wanted to see himself in shackles again or eating beef jerky or cutting cane at dawn. That was why they went to war. And they didn't want to stay behind either because an old black man who didn't go to war was left all alone and couldn't survive. He died broken-hearted. The African blacks were friendly, jokesters, story tellers, rogues.

They weren't going to plant their butts in a barracoon without talking to anybody!

Many of them followed their sons or their grandsons into the ranks. They were put under the command of the officers, who were criollos. They became morning sentries, they did guard duty, they cooked, they washed, they cleaned the weapons...All of those chores were appropriate for them. There was no bozal who was an officer in the war. In my squadron, commanded by Higinio Esquerra,[17] there were three or four of them. One was named Jaime, another Santiago. They were both Congos. I can't remember which of them, I think the oldest, passed the time saying, "Ussens not fraid of da war. Ussens used to it. In Africa ussens fight a lot." Thing is that they had factions fighting over there. Men and women fought. They killed each other in those disputes. It was like what happened here in the barrios of Havana, in Jesus María, in Belén, in Manglar...The ñáñigos fought amongst themselves in that African way. It's the same thing. You can't say they were savages because the whites who got involved with the ñáñigo movement also practiced that custom.

If the Africans didn't know what they were getting into, the Cubans didn't either. Most of them, I mean. What was happening was that there was a revolution around here, a fine mess everybody fell into. Even the most cagey ones. People were saying, "Cuba Libre! Down with Spain!" Then they said, "Long live the King!" Who knows! That was an inferno. The solution wasn't to be seen anywhere. There was only one way out, and it was war.

At first no one explained the Revolution. You got into it because you wanted to. I myself didn't think about the future. The only thing I said was, "Cuba Libre!" The leaders went around getting people together and explaining it to them. They talked to all the battalions. First, they said they were proud to be Cubans, and the Grito de Baire[18] had united us. They urged the people to fight, and said they were real certain that we would win. How many people thought the whole thing was just a fiesta for winning prizes! When they came under fire they ran away. They betrayed their brothers. There were many of that stripe. Others stood firm. A thing that lifted our spirits was the speech Maceo gave at Mal Tiempo. He said, "It's a war for independence now. When we are through, each soldier will be paid thirty pesos."

That was all I heard. And it was true. The war ended, and they paid me 982 pesos. Everything Maceo said was true. He was the greatest man of the war. He said nobody would be a loser because we were all going to be free. And that's just how it was. At least I didn't lose. Not even my health. I have a bullet in my thigh, and I can still lift up my pant leg and see the black mark. But there were those who didn't even make it out of the forest. They went from the top of the horse to under the ground.

To tell the truth, the war was necessary. The dead were going to die anyway, and without helping anyone. I remained alive by pure chance. It seems my mission hadn't been completed. The gods give each of us a task...Today I can talk about all of this, and laugh about it, but being under fire, watching people dying all around, and the bullets and the cannons and—that was different. The war was necessary. It wasn't fair that so many jobs and so many privileges happened to fall into the hands of the Spaniards alone. It wasn't fair that for women to work they had to be daughters of Spaniards. None of that was fair. You never saw a black lawyer because they said that blacks were only good for the forest. You never saw a black teacher. It was all for the white Spaniards. Even the white criollos were pushed aside. I seen that myself. A night watchman, whose only job was to walk around, call out the hour, and put out a candle, had to be a Spaniard. And everything was like that. There was no freedom. That's why a war was necessary. I realized it when the leaders explained the situation. The reason why you had to fight.

THE WAR OF INDEPENDENCE

Life During the War

I came to join up in the War on the third or fourth of December in 95. I was at the Ariosa, and informed about everything. One day I met with my oldest friends at the sugarmill, and I told them we had to rise up. So then we went full into it. The one who went with me first was Juan Fábregas. He was a good looking, decisive black man. I hardly had to say a word to him. He guessed what I had in mind. We left the mill in the afternoon and walked until we came to a small farm. There we grabbed the first horses we saw, tied up to some trees. It wasn't stealing. I made the effort to tell the farmer in proper language: "Please give me the complete outfit, saddle and all." He gave it all to me with bits and spurs, and without a pause, put it on the horse. I was ready for battle. I didn't carry firearms. A machete was enough for those times. I rode fast on the main thoroughfares. I almost got to Camagüey.

When I came across the Mambises troops, I shouted, and they saw me and the men who were with me. From that day on I gave myself entirely over to the War. Unexpectedly, I felt pretty confused. It's true that whole thing was a terrible mess. They hadn't even formed squadrons or appointed officers. But there was discipline even under these conditions. We were never lacking for blockhead little soldiers or bandits. But it was the same in the war of 68, so I've been told.

From Camagüey I came down with the columns toward Las Villas. Things were already different because when you're united, you have more confidence. I went around making friends so as not to put people off, and by the time we got to Mal Tiempo everyone knew me, by sight at least. Fábregas was better than I was about making friends. He won the men over right away. He told stories and joked around like the devil himself. Before getting to Mal Tiempo, there wasn't a single engagement I hadn't been involved in.

Mal Tiempo was my first taste of the War. It was the first hell the Spaniards suffered in Cuba. Long before we got there, the leaders knew what would happen. They warned us about it to get us ready. And that's how it was. The devil was inside all of us when we got there. The machete was the weapon of the day. The officers told us: "When we get there, raise your machetes high."

Maceo directed the battle. From the beginning he was at the front. Máximo Gómez assisted him, and together they carried the day. Máximo Gómez was brave but reserved. He had a lot of complicated schemes. I never trusted him. The proof of that came much later. The proof of his disloyalty to Cuba. But that's a horse of a different color.

At Mal Tiempo we had to stick together, and you had to follow the man who rolled up his sleeves and raised up his machete. Mal Tiempo lasted maybe half an hour, but it was enough to cause more deaths than an inferno. More Spaniards fell there than in all the battles fought later. It was a flat, open field, a clearing, a plain. Those who were used to fighting on hillsides had their troubles there. At Mal Tiempo there was a tiny bunch of houses, surrounded by ravines, creeks, and many stands of pineapple. When the slaughter ended, we could see mounds of little Spanish heads along the fence of the pineapple grove. I've seen few things more striking than that.

When we got to Mal Tiempo, Maceo gave the order to fight face to face. And that's how it was done. The Spaniards, from the moment they saw us, went stiff all over. They thought we came armed with short carbines and Mausers. But, shit, what we did was to take some shafts of wild guava and carry them under our arms to scare them. They went crazy when they saw us, and they threw themselves into the thick of it, but the fight didn't last long because at almost the same instant, we started to chop off their heads. But really chopping them off. The Spaniards were scared shitless of the machetes. They weren't afraid of rifles but machetes, yes. I raised mine, and from a distance said: "You bastard, now I'm going to cut your head off." Then the starched little soldier turned tail immediately and took off. Since I had no criminal instincts, I would let him go. Even so, I had to cut off some heads. Especially when I saw that one of them was coming at me. Some were brave, the minority, and they had to be eliminated. Generally, I asked them for their Mauser. I said: "Hold it up." They would answer: "Listen, you bastard, if you want my Mauser, just take it." They threw a lot of Mausers in my face. Fact is they were real cowards.

Others did the same because they were naive, very young. The conscripts, for example, were sixteen to eighteen years old. They came fresh from Spain and had never fought before. When they found themselves in a jam, they were capable of dropping everything, even their pants. I ran into many of them at Mal Tiempo. Later, too, because they did fight in the War. I think there were too many of them in Spain, so they were sent off to war.

The fiercest battalion to fight at Mal Tiempo was from the Canary Islands. They were well equipped. Almost all of them died from the same fear of the machete. They didn't obey their commander. They threw themselves on the ground from fright. They dropped their rifles, and they even hid behind trees. Even with all that crap, they were the ones who put their shoulders into the fight. The tactic they used was pretty smart, but once we destroyed it, they were goners. They formed what they called squares and dug holes in the ground from which to shoot. They knelt there, forming a line of fixed bayonets. Sometimes it worked, and sometimes not.

Mal Tiempo was the defeat of that tactic. The first moments were hard for us. Then, their squares in confusion, they had no choice but to shoot at will They tried to bayonet our horses and the riders shot them to pieces They seemed crazed. They were scattered all over. That was a horrible confusion. Fear was their greatest enemy.

To tell the truth, we Cubans acquitted ourselves well. I myself seen many Mambises who rose above the bullets. The bullets were like puffs of cotton to us. What was important was the ideal, the things we had to defend, like everything that Maceo talked about, and even Máximo Gómez, though he never carried any of them out. Mal Tiempo shook up the Cubans. It animated their spirits and gave them strength.

They tried to kill me at Mal Tiempo. It was a Galician who saw me in the distance and aimed at me. I grabbed him by the throat and spared his life. A few minutes later he was killed. What I did was take away his ammunition and his rifle, maybe his clothes, I don't remember. I don't think I did because our uniform wasn't too bad. That Galician looked at me, and said: "You're savages." Then he set off running, and they killed him. Of course they thought we were savages, them being so timid. Besides, they came here for something completely different. They had been figuring that the war was a game. So when the game got rough, they began to fall back. They started to think we were animals, not

men—that's how they came to call us Mambises. Mambí
means the child of a monkey and a buzzard. It was a
taunting phrase, but we used it in order to cut off their
heads. At Mal Tiempo they realized that. So much so that
the Mambí became a lion. That was seen at Mal Tiempo
better than anywhere else. Everything happened there. It
was the worst slaughter of the War. It happened that way
because it was predestined. There are things you can't
change. The course of life is very complicated. ┌ᴇᴏ⌐ᴄ⫏

Mal Tiempo was necessary to give courage to the Cubans
and to give strength to the revolution. Anyone who fought
there left convinced he could face the enemy. Maceo
repeated it many times on the road and in the fields. Because
Maceo was certain of victory. He always felt that way. He
didn't waver or let up. He was tougher than a hardwood
tree. If Maceo hadn't fought there, things would have been
different. We would have committed suicide.

The Spaniards said that he and his brother José were
criminals. That's a lie. He was not a supporter of killing. He
killed for the ideal, but I never heard him say that a man's
head should be chopped off. Others said it and did it every
day. It's also true that death was necessary. You can't go to
war and just cross your arms because that's the role of the
sissy.

Maceo acted like a real man at Mal Tiempo. He was
always at the front. He had an Arabian horse that was even
braver than he was. It seemed that nothing could slow him
down. After the Spanish volley began, and they were all
stretched out on the ground with bayonets in place, he
approached the squadron I was in, and that's where I seen
him best. The firing had died down a little. You could still
hear some shots. Maceo was tall, stout, had mustaches, and
was a talker. He gave orders, and then was the first to carry

them out. I never seen him give a soldier the flat of his blade. Not once. Now, every now and then he did whip the backside of those Colonels who acted rebellious. He used to say that the common soldier was not to blame for their mistakes.

Besides Maceo and Gómez, there were some real sharp men. Quintín Banderas was one. He was as black as coal, but only Maceo was more fiery. Quintín fought in the other war, in 68. He had the spirit for that. Maybe he enjoyed it. He was a bitter man. I've been told that he went to the wars to fight for the blacks. Well, people talk a lot of foolishness, too. In any case, the blacks were his supporters. I myself had a lot of faith in him. I seen him on several occasions. At Mal Tiempo and later. He came to Mal Tiempo late and with few men. He'd had some skirmishes just before. He arrived with two mules, two women, and a handful of men, very few. The Spanish were scared to death of him. They didn't even want to see a picture of him. He was always playing with their heads—he eluded them, he made fun of them, and then when he caught one outright, he beheaded him. He would ask him: "What's your name?" and when the Spaniard was about to say his name, Quintín answered: "You done did have that name," and cut off his head.

Banderas had a problem with Máximo Gómez at Mal Tiempo. I don't know why it was, but the whole troop noticed it. Then they had another and another and yet another. One time Banderas was returning to Mal Tiempo with his men, and he had to fight in the battle of La Olayita, near Rodrigo. He nearly lost his entire command. He put up great resistance but came out badly. It was because of a cane break there. The horses got stuck and made an immense mud hole, a...So they accused him, I don't know who, of going to surrender to the Spanish. The accusation was due to the hatred of blacks. It's true there were black partisans and snitches, but Banderas' good points were all anyone could talk about. Máximo Gómez wanted to place him under the command of Carrillo, who wasn't a general or anything close to it. Later Maceo cleared the matter up, and Quintín returned to fight with his men.

I've seen brave men, but only Quintín was like Maceo. He had many jobs in the Republic, but he was never given a good opportunity. The bust that they made of him was abandoned on the docks for many years. The bust of a patriot. That's why people are still riled up. Because of the lack of respect for the true liberators. If you tell people about that bust, they think it's a lie. And still, I seen it. I don't know where it could be now. Maybe they set it up again.

I would make ten busts of Banderas. One for every battle. He deserves it. At Mal Tiempo he wiped out a whole bunch of Canary Islanders. I think Banderas himself downed half those Spaniards. And did they fall, hundreds of them! The whole field was full of bodies, the paths, the boundary lanes between properties, everywhere. The Mambises themselves took carts and wagon loads of the dead to Cruces. I didn't take part in that. I had enough to do with the ones who had fallen beside me, blown apart.

After the victory we got ready to keep marching on. With more spirit now than ever. I remember we were still disorganized, and we had frequent arguments and scuffles over leadership. They hadn't formed squadrons yet. In fact, we were adrift. What there was in abundance was the will to fight but there was no organization. Maceo and Gómez were the main leaders, but they couldn't control all of their command. I think the first place we went to was the Las Nieves mill. We got arms and supplies there and went straight off then towards La Olayita, where we fought together with Banderas in that mud bath of a ravine. The enemy was well-positioned there. Our horses slipped, the sons of bitches, and all hell broke loose. Then we arrived at El Mamey. There was heavy fighting at El Mamey. We were united in that battle. The Spanish put up some resistance, but we taught them another lesson. We went on to other plantations. We were nearing Matanzas, and still with no established leaders. We passed by the España and Hatuey plantations. We were carrying a whole load of weapons. About that time, Máximo Gómez and Cayito Alvarez began to appoint leaders and form mobile squadrons. It was a hard time. Not everyone was happy with their commanders. No one rebelled, out of decency, but we were given some real little brutes of officers. I was assigned to Tajó, the highwayman and bandit. I knew him well. It bothered me to have to obey his orders, but there was no other way. In war you can't question things, you have to follow orders. Tajó pitched his camp on the El Capitolio hill, a stupid little hill between Jicotea, San Diego and Esperanza. The camp was next to a ceiba tree. There was a thicket behind it, and below an empty field. The camp wasn't very big although it was kept well supplied. It was hard to get up there. You had to climb a hill covered with grasses and brush. No Spaniard ever dared. Tajó spent hours saying: "No Spaniard will climb up here. Not a single fucking one!" He would pace around in circles and laugh. He was meaner than all of us put together. He wanted to make the camp into a front line. Of course, we knew all the entrances and exits to and from the camp. One of the easiest ways in was through the estate's main entrance. It was a gateway called "The Red Door." We entered through there and all of Tajó's men and women friends, too.

Tajó began to be great friends with a guy named Daniel Fuentes. He was a Cuban and pretended to be the Spanish scout in that zone. They were old friends from peace time. I never liked the man, as I kept telling Juan Fábregas, the one from the Ariosa who joined up with me. Juan was very calm, and he never replied. But I kept on having my doubts. At first I thought Tajó wanted to surrender. Then I realized that wasn't it, that what was happening was that Daniel informed Tajó about all of the Spaniard's maneuvers. That's why we were never discovered or fired upon.

Every time a partisan or an enemy column was going to pass by, Daniel would send word. I didn't like him because that kind of man can turn any which way. Today he's with me and the next with the other guy. Tajó never dared to talk to me about it because I knew how he operated. It always seemed to me he was up to no good. I could see it in his eyes. When I saw that the sentry left his post, and nobody said anything I knew then that Daniel Fuentes had loosened his tongue. Tajó himself gave the order to remove the watch. The whole troop waited in silence, and at a distance we watched the Spanish pass by, all starched, on their Arabian horses. In any case it would have been hard to see us. Our camp was clean, it didn't even have any garbage around. Everyone slept on the ground. Other soldiers made their place to sleep with Guinea grass and reeds.

Tajó had other informants. Among them were Felipe el Sol, who was later informant to Cayito Alvarez and perhaps someone else's. I condemn those men. They're like puppets without heads. Well, Felipe el Sol did save our lives several times. Even so I didn't trust him. His favorite game was to walk among the troops bragging. No one paid him any mind. I never even looked at him. I kept on telling Fábregas that that guy was a bastard.

While I was with Tajó, there were no casualties. There were forty men when I went in. When I left there was the same number. The mobile squadrons were not very heavily equipped, which is why there were called mobile. Besides, they had no base camp. All the personnel they had was quick-witted. We probably did many foolish things since we had no military discipline or any knowledge of war. We got to the point where we could take off at night, one, two, or three men, sometimes with the Captain's permission, or Tajó's. And we used to go to the neighboring farms where we would steal big sixty or eighty pound piglets. The Madrazos farm was the biggest and best because it had a special way of raising pigs. We left late, around ten at night. We left on horseback, and we caught the pigs from our horses because they were pretty wild. They ran loose. They didn't have to be given any feed. We fell in behind the first one we saw. For us it was a game, and from up on the horse, after we had tired him out, we would give him a good slash on the leg with the machete. The pig's foot would go flying off, and he couldn't go on running. We jumped off quickly and grabbed him by the neck. The bad part of that was that the pig bled all over and squealed a lot.

On account of that squealing we were ambushed once. They didn't catch us, but it was a big scare. The next night we went straight back to the same spot, just because. There were no more than four of us. No one saw us, or at least they pretended to be fooled. We continued to go back and stole more each time. We never again heard a shot. I think they were afraid of us. They understood that every night different group of us went, and they were frightened.

I was with Tajó for a few months. One day I had had enough, and I left. He had gone too far. The tricks and lies were a daily occurrence. He stole oxen, cattle, he sold teams of oxen to just about anybody, well...a complete disaster. Tajó was a horse thief in a liberator's uniform. There were a lot of others like him.

The day I'm talking about, José, his brother, who fought alongside him in the war, came to me looking strange and said to me: "Hey, Esteban, don't say a word but come help me bury Cañón." Cañón was a brave young man in the group. It chilled me to hear that. I only managed to say: "What! Cañón is dead?" He said yes, and not to ask so many questions. Later that shameless bastard tried to explain: "Cañón stole a lot, man. You can't do anything with a thief like that..."

I found Cañón hanging fom a rope as thick as my arm. It sounded like a lie to me—I knew Cañón was honest. Within two days I found out the whole thing was over a woman. A woman who came to see Cañón every night. Tajó fell in love with her, even though he already had a woman, and so he killed Cañón. I ran over to where Juan was, and said to him: "Juan, I'm leaving. Cayito is at El Plátano, a short ways away." Juan didn't fail me. He followed me to El Plátano, and there we put ourselves under the command of Cayito Alvarez. Three months after I ran away from Tajó, I learned that he had surrendered to the Spanish, to that party that wanted home rule you heard so much talk about. It was just what you would expect from him. He took things so casually that after turning himself over, he escaped and went back to the liberator's side. Good Lord, what dirty tricks!

Those were the kinds of men who waged the war. For good or ill, but it was fought. They stripped him of his captain's bars, but he went on acting the same way. There isn't much difference between buck private and captain.

They accused him of many crimes. He found himself in a real hell of a mess.

When the war ended, I saw him in El Sapo, a little farm where he lived near La Esperanza. He must have been sixty then. I said hello, and he greeted me, and asked me to come in. He didn't remind me once of my deserting him. He was aware I knew his weak spots. He made me a gift of a fine gamecock which I later sold.

Tajó must be dead. Hell is too good for a man like him, but that must be where he is. A man who kept having sex with his daughters, who didn't even let them get married, and who screwed up so much in the war, has to be in hell.

It was the same with Cayito. I noticed it right from the beginning. And as time went on it became even clearer. Cayito was a colonel. You could say he was handsome and decisive. His entire regiment had a tough character. A special kind of discipline, iron hard on Cayito's part. I don't think it was the best thing. Sometimes a soft touch is needed. Those men who think they're more powerful than God make a mistake, and he made that mistake. The first day I arrived there I figured out what kind of man that Cayito was. That son of a bitch! A sergeant named Félix turned to him and said: "Colonel, here are some men from that screw-up Tajó. Cayito looked us up and down, we signed the enlistment papers, and we didn't say a word. Taking it all in, I heard Cayito: "I expected as much from Tajó. I've known for some time he was going to trip up. He was mixed up in one dirty deal after another."

He said it all with those few words. And what a way to say it. With the coldness of the one who sees a crime and covers it up. Just my luck. To go from one thief to another thief, from one murderer to another murderer. Anyone who fought with Cayito can swear to it. He had the head of the first man who disobeyed him. If it had been up to him, this island would be one big cemetery.

In that regiment there was no stepping out of line. If Cayito walked by some soldier and just glanced at him, the soldier had the shakes for hours. There was little difference between Cayito and Tajó. Very little. Both of them were murderous types who hooked up with the war. They probably knew each other well. At least Cayito frequently talked about Tajó, nothing good to say, of course.

Even with all the talk, Cayito was the calmer of the two. Tajó was a more spirited adventurer. Cayito liked strategies and Tajó liked violence. I know it because I was with the both of them. There was more fighting with Cayito, or I should say, more hand to hand combat. To tell the truth, the war wasn't so hard with either one of them. The worst for me was Mal Tiempo, the most tragic experience. Of the encounters we had with Spanish troops, there are two of some importance. Although importance is an elastic thing. I say important because there was shooting and danger, and we saved our hides. For other liberators maybe they were just fun and games. But you always remember the times when your own life and limb are hanging by a thread.

At one of those encounters Cayito himself was in command. He lead with a firm hand, but he was arrogant. When danger was close, he played with his mustaches as if he was curling them. It was an obsession with him, typical of a man with character.

He wouldn't leave camp for anything. That led some who didn't know him to label him a coward. There are still people who say bad things about Cayito. Ignorant people who deny his bravery. You can say what you like about him about him, but he wasn't bashful Some people also say he was rather short, plump and dark. They didn't know him, you see, because he was tall, skinny, and fair-skinned, so you shouldn't pay much attention to what people say. Making things up is another bad habit. I complained about him all the time, calling him a murderer and a bandit. But he was no coward. Few men were as decisive as he was in the thick of battle. He always defeated the Spanish with his strategy of using bombs. Fact is, he placed a few at the entrance to the camp and had them set off every time some partisans approached. Those explosions scared the soldiers off immediately. Their horses ran away so fast it made the horseshoes smoke. In the first battle I fought under Cayito, he used those bombs. Bombs with spools of wire that extended some fifty feet. The look-out signaled if he saw someone coming. A shot in the air was enough. The one with the detonator jumped up and took it by the handle, got ready, and shoved it down hard. Within a few seconds, it seemed as if the world was coming to an end. There were mean screaming, horses bolting, horribly wounded, legs dangling from trees, and pieces of heads scattered on the ground, that looked all dried up a few days later. There was a stench because when the dead aren't buried, they raise a terrible stink. The Spanish were really afraid of the bombs. That was the reason for Cayito's success in the war.

This first fighting was easy. We had wiped out a group of conscripts who came up to us to nose around. The second fight was more difficult. All the cards were on the table there. A convoy for Manicaragua was coming from God knows where. The convoy was heavily loaded, and the only way through was past us. They had to cross the El Plátano plantation at any cost. An informer let us know it was coming, and Cayito called out the troops to say: "Now you have to fight like lions." No one got scared right then. On the contrary, our desire to fight increased. Cayito went on giving orders. He laid out a big firing line and brought the infantry up close. He looked out at the people coming and went walking back to camp. He was going along laughing. A few seconds later you could hear the shouting. Cayito shouted like a beast. The convoy was trapped. We took some prisoners and confiscated weapons, food, rice, lard, bacon, ham, everything. We ate like kings for days and days. Not only us, the women too, the officers' women. Cayito had his own woman nearby. Her name was María, and she lived in a pretty decent hut, that's for sure. Many was the time I myself took food to her.

We kept the Spanish soldiers prisoner there. No one talked to them. Some wanted to kill them, but there was who-knows-what order that prohibited the killing of prisoners of war. Cayito didn't share that view of things. He would have wiped them out right away. He said to them under his breath: "You deserve to die, you bastards." They were all quiet because they were youngsters and were afraid of us. We gave them no food, but after three days we let them go. We sent them to town with one or two pairs of men as guards.

At El Plátano there were no more engagements. It seems Cayito frightened them away. That man's spirit was something else. He was stronger than his whole regiment. Nobody ever rebelled against him. Still, there were few people who didn't know about the horrible things he did. The town of Cruces knew well enough that he killed his own soldiers. He killed his own father-in-law in order to carry off the man's wife. He took her and killed him. Now there are people who think that's funny. To me it's a crime.

One time Cayito buried something at El Plátano. He had a passion for hiding money, pots full of gold. Where he buried it remains a mystery. Nobody has been able to dig it up. Cayito took his adjutant with him to bury the money and then killed him with his own hands. Some say he buried him right there. I don't know. The thing was that after a few days he walked around a little worried. He became solemn and downhearted. I was told it was because he thought one of his men had seen the spot where he buried the money. Those were uneasy days in the camp. I myself thought, all right, if this man thinks I seen the burying of the money and his adjutant, he's going to knock me into the same hole.

After a few days passed, calm returned. A fair-skinned mulatto got the field stocks during that time, but it was for other reasons. The field stocks was the devil's punishment. Cayito used it on everyone who didn't swallow his ideas.

I got the field stocks once. Because of an officer I disobeyed. I left my watch without telling him, and he punished me. He called me in and said: "Listen, Esteban, you have no discipline." I answered him back because I wasn't going to be quiet. The truth be told, I don't know what I said to him. Right off things got all mixed up. That bum called two aides and tied my hands with a rope to make sure I didn't escape. Then he tied a carbine between my knees so my legs couldn't move. He had me like that for a whole day. I saw stars from the pain. And come to think about it, I didn't come off so bad. A soldier who abandons a post is called a deserter in the field, I mean, a traitor, and he often gets hanged. I was saved, but I still go around thinking about that man's mother.

Later on, he and I were on the lookout for each other. He took the watch with me because he thought I was a rebel. Any time he could, he kept me in camp. He knew my

pleasure was to go out at night to steal pigs and cattle. I was
an expert hand in those operations. Cayito himself knew it.

Well, that officer kept me in camp every now and again
just to annoy me. And it did annoy me a lot because for me
not to go out was like being in prison. I think the thing I did
best during the war was stealing livestock. Since we couldn't
plant any crops, we stole cattle. You had to look for food
somehow. The one who did that job gained respect. Cayito
one day called me over, and said: "Negro, you're already
bringing us food, so be one of my bodyguards." I never
answered him. I just started to follow new orders. More
direct than the ones before. So I went out every night and
came back with such good calves and pigs it was a marvel.
Some wild and some tame. Someone always went with me. A
man couldn't do that work by himself.

There were some places where you could have a garden.
In Las Villas, not even on a bet. Camagüey was a quiet place.
There was hardly any fighting there. The soldiers sowed
crops and even had 'taters. There were farms and big rich
people's houses where no Spanish soldier ever went. That
was the province that had seen the least fighting. In Las
Villas it was different. There the Spanish burned the houses
of the revolutionaries, and their partisans took over large
areas of land. And that's not just a wild tale because I seen it
with my own eyes.

The most a revolutionary could do in Las Villas was to
steal livestock collect taro weeds, sweet potato shoots,
amaranth, purslane, and such. Mango flour was made by
cooking mango pulp without the pit. You added lemon and
hot guaguao pepper. That was the food we had in the war.
The rest was nonsense. Oh! And lots of curujey juice. Being

thirsty was a constant thing. During war hunger goes away, but thirst, never.

The horses got skinny. They got old quick. You couldn't give them curujey water. Taking them to a stream was the only solution. Truth is that one of the troop's biggest problems was water. It was the same for everyone. That's why the officers looked for a way to make camp near a river. And I know of cases where sentries left their posts. They ran off to get water. When they came back, they got the field stocks. I never did that, but I often felt like it.

The soldiers were a mixed bag. Good men and scoundrels. I had few friends. Juan and Santiago were the closest because they left the Ariosa with me. Though I didn't sympathize much with Santiago. He was a little blood-thirsty and stiff-necked. He never showed me any disrespect, but he did hide many things from me. I found out about his tricks from his own brother. Santiago was clumsy. He shouted "Cuba Libre!" till he was hoarse. One day he got tired of Cayito, and without saying a word either to his brother or to me, he took off. A little while later we learned he had made the stupid mistake of turning himself over to the Spanish in the tiny town of Jicotea. When he got there, those same Spaniards accused him of killing a Galician who was cutting herbs in the forest. That caught him by surprise, and he was speechless, unable to defend himself. They immediately sentenced him to death. They shot him in the head and hung him in front of a thatched hut that they burned down afterwards. That served as a warning to Cubans who were uncertain about their loyalties. I'll always remember that incident. It still makes me angry.

There were lots of men like Santiago. So, you couldn't even trust your friends. If they had forced him to talk, I'm sure he would have spilled everything. But they didn't even give him the chance.

The best thing for war times is not to trust anybody. The same for peacetime, though in war it's even more necessary. You have to distrust men. That's not sad because it's true. There are good men and scoundrels. The difficulty is knowing the one from the other. I've gotten mixed up a number of times in my life.

Cayito Alvarez wouldn't even trust his own mother. He was right. He had enemies. Almost all his men were his enemies deep down. They saw what he did, his robberies, his killings, and, naturally, they had to hate him. During the war, there were many upstanding men, who hated quietly, with the deepest hate there is.

While I served with him, I watched him closely. He was one of those men who celebrated when new troops arrived. When someone came to join up, he would call him over and talk with him. Sometimes he told the man to go to another commander. He did that when he realized the man was not trustworthy. What interested him were men who would keep quiet about his crimes and wrongdoing. I say it now quite freely, but I was almost a prisoner then.

Cayito reached the point where he turned whole groups away. There were times when an officer was wounded, and the group was without a commander. Then they had to be sent to another regiment. At El Plátano that happened often. Men would arrive, and we detained them. Sometimes they stayed, others danced off with the music to some other place. Whenever a group approached, we gave them the order to halt: "Halt, the officer of the group will step forward." One stepped forward, identified himself, and if the outfit was big, we sent for the officer of the day, who was authorized by the

Sergeant Major to allow him to pass. Meanwhile our troops kept the newcomers covered, just in case. As the minutes passed, tensions eased up, friends shook hands, sometimes relatives met, and that was how an outfit joined the regiment.

If the officers agreed, they were sent to be enlisted, and after that they belonged. That's how many men got in to fight alongside of Cayito. I think the same thing happened in other places and with other officers. They weren't going to let anyone in just for the fun of it. The war was serious business, and not everybody was loyal. I heard it said that some partisans who passed for Mambises snuck into a squadron from Matanzas. That business ended up bloody and ugly. That was why so many precautions were taken.

The Captains and Colonels themselves quarreled among themselves. Out of envy, out of hypocrisy and out of hate. That bickering brought many deaths for Cuba, much blood. Not everyone who went to war had the stomach for it. When some saw the lit fuse, they panicked and beat a retreat. Even the colonels. The death of Maceo weakened the morale to fight. In those days a good number of officers turned themselves over to Spain. That's the lowest thing a man could do, the dirtiest. Surrender to Spain in the Cuban jungle! That was the limit!

Cayito himself wanted to do it. That dirty bastard kept it secret although many already suspected it. Me too, to tell the truth. But since he was so animal-like, so ferocious, no one talked about it so as to not end up in trouble. I can just imagine the unfortunate soul who might have started that rumor during those days. Cayito would have eaten him alive. In little bites. Luckily everyone kept quiet about that. The real show went on behind the scenes. Felipe el Sol was the one who revealed it all. He was the kind for doing such a thing. I never seen him or heard him that day, but I do know that he went over to where Leonardo Fuentes was and a guy named Remigio Pedroso from Cayito's guard, and said to them: "I know on good authority that your man is going to surrender." Seeing as how they were revolutionaries and tough, they reacted well. They went over to some men they knew to be trustworthy, what we called loyal, and they told them the news. Everybody was tense but ready.

They waited for few days for Felipe el Sol to return. Finally, after a week he appeared to say that the Spanish columns were going to approach the following morning to get Cayito and a few of his loyal followers. We immediately got together a group of us and decided to have Remigio kill Cayito at a specified time. Just then Remigio appeared with his eyes bulging wide, and said: "Cayito took me aside and ordered me to inform you that he was going to surrender. I kept quiet and promised to carry out his orders. Also, he told me that they were going to give him the sum of fifteen thousand pesos which he was going to share, and he would be recognized as a colonel in the Spanish army. I congratulated him, and here I am to do whatever you order me to do." After we heard that, we decided that Remigio had to be the one to kill Cayito after all.

Remigio agreed. The Spaniards were going to arrive at seven in the morning. At that hour Remigio was ready and instead of announcing that Cayito was going to surrender, he was to take him to a stand of mango trees, which should be still there today, to kill him.

Day dawned brightly. General Duque was approaching. He was in charge of the Spanish column that would take Cayito into the Autonomous State. Other Cuban Colonels had already surrendered. Cayito was not going to be the only one to surrender. Vicente Núñez and Joaquín Macagua, from other regiments, arrived to surrender with him. The three of them met up a long ways from El Plátano. Cayito's guard followed him. Naturally, I went with them. Remigio had been prepared for some time already. He lead Cayito and the other two Colonels to the mango grove. Meeting there together, we had them dead to rights. There are some who say that the one who killed Cayito was Leonardo Fuentes, a black man in his guard. Others say that Remigio himself did it, as was planned. The truth is very difficult to prove. Cayito took three bullets, each fatal. The killers had hidden behind some bushes. When they heard Cayito talking treason with the other two Colonels, they turned his chest into a sieve.

That was the end of Cayito. Later the liars and the storytellers came who say that he put up a fight and was as brave as a lion. Not a bit of it. He fell down without even a sigh. The Spaniards discovered there had been trouble at the camp and didn't send out any columns that day. The next morning Felipe el Sol arrived. He came to see for sure. Since he was a spy for the Cubans, he already figured it out. So he went back to General Duque, pretending to cry, and informed him teary-eyed about Cayito's death. Felipe had a knack for that kind of work.

The Spanish came out to the camp. Many of Cayito's men had already moved on. Others remained hidden to see what would happen. I seen it all, and then I lit out of there. The Spaniards came and held up the flag. They got down from their horses, and one took out a paper, and said: "An officer has died trying to honor the Spanish flag." That's what happened. Anyone who says otherwise is wrong. These kinds of things happened in war, which is why I say it destroys men's ability to trust.

Thinking it over, Cayito didn't do any more than follow the example of other officers. They didn't consider it treason to surrender during that time because it was said that since Maceo had died, the revolution was lost. Maybe Cayito surrendered because of Maceo's death. He admired him. But no, Cayito was pig tripe, a traitor.

There are still people who talk about Cayito. They hope to see him somewhere. That's because they didn't know him. If they had known him, they wouldn't have his name on the tip of their tongues. What I'm talking about are those lights that come out at night in the hills. And the headless horseman. Many say that's the spirit of Cayito going out to watch over the money he hid away. Perhaps it is Cayito. I don't want to even think about him. Let it be somebody else!

One day an old negro came to tell me he saw lights, and that those lights were the soul of the bandolero Cayito Alvarez. He was scared. I looked at him, and I kept my trap shut. In the end I wasn't going to convince him of anything. On the inside I did think, well, this fool didn't know him alive and didn't fight side by side with him. If he had been at his side in life, he wouldn't have been scared of him dead. The way he was really fierce was when he was alive.

After the death of Cayito a large group of us, those of us from his regiment, set off in the direction of a spot called Tranca to hide. Night came on us there. In Morota, a tiny barrio near La Esperanza, we slept till the next day. We hadn't gotten to El Plátano, where the infantry and the Mauser squadron were camped, made up of brave black men. When we arrived a great commotion started up. All the men, around six hundred, asked us what had happened. We told them about the deaths of Cayito, Macagua and

Núñez. They froze up. There were happy and confused both.

We organized ourselves, and the remaining officers gave the order to set out to join up with Brigadier Higinio Esquerra. I had already heard talk of him. All of the officers were mentioned. Some knew more, some knew less about what they were like, how they treated their men, and other details. Then there was gossip about women, and whether this officer or that one was a bandit or a decent guy. So that when they gave the order, everyone thought to themselves: off to fight with another bandit! I didn't think that way myself. After all, even a bandit could go straight.

I no sooner than saw Higinio's face than I knew. He was a man of few words. He liked action better. As soon as we arrived he asked us some questions. I didn't offer an answer because I thought I didn't have the right. I seen him balanced and decisive. His sideburns were unmistakable because he was very white, a country man like thousands, thin and tall. He took charge right off. With a confidence that left everyone more or less flat footed.

The first thing he did was to call a court martial for a certain Espinosa, Cayito's brother-in-law, who we had taken prisoner because the coward was going to surrender. Espinosa didn't think Higinio was going to treat him that way. Perhaps he thought it was a tea party. I remember that the last thing Espinosa asked was that someone take his handsome silver watch to his mother. Higinio himself took the watch and sent it to her. He had traits like that, a lettuce among the cabbages.

Later, early in the afternoon, he delivered a ringing speech to the troops. He did this to inspire them. He explained the whole story. He said Cayito was a traitor, and that other men were mixed up in the business. The men looked each other over from head to foot. Many knew there was a cat in the bag. Higinio read Cayito's private papers. He read them out loud. I never witnessed such silence—above all, when he began to read the names of the people involved. He spoke the names clearly, each one's name and rank. Many little colonels were named on that list. Colonels who didn't turn themselves in out of fear.

The conduct of our troops was a model for the others, as anyone will tell you who fought in the war. That's why we saw the Revolution through. I'm certain that almost all the troops would have done the same in that situation. We were brave and put the revolution above everything else. That's the truth. Even so, many colonels and other officers shit off-target every day. They did things that not even little children do.

To gain the respect of a brigadier you had to be a man who was very straight and very dependable. The Brigadier was gruff and treated people sharply, but he permitted no treachery. I respected him a great deal because there was something noble about him. He sent a group of us, a commission, to General Máximo Gómez. He said the commission was to be made up of brave and loyal men. Men who had stood up during the business with Cayito. It's true that in that commission there were real soldiers, men who hadn't backed down. But it was a small group. More should have gone. You could count on your fingers the ones who went: Lieutenant Primitivo del Portal, Captain Leonardo Fuentes, Major Zúñigas, Corporal Hugo Cuéllar, and Second Lieutenant Remigio Pedroso. They got in to see Máximo Gómez, who at that time was at La Campana. Máximo Gómez greeted them and talked with them. Later, for their action he promoted each one in rank. In my opinion, the troop deserved a medal because everyone had helped in the revolt. There were a lot of us, though, and they couldn't decorate us all.

The officers returned within a few days, each with his new rank, and they had to be officially welcomed. I'm still not convinced that Máximo Gómez understood clearly how Cayito died. For my part, I think they told him only some of it, what was good for them. Each one of them wanted to make his mark, too. Besides, people thought Cayito's death was because of racism. Officers of other battalions, that is, because those in the know realized which side was up. But at the time of the decision, the officers were united. They said: "Yes, yes, yes."

When the war ended, I heard many people said, and say even now: "The blacks were against Cayito, they killed him." You have to keep quiet or tell the truth. But since so few people believe you, well then, you keep quiet. And if you don't, it becomes complicated, or rather it did, because today nobody puts up with people running off at the mouth.

Higinio didn't ever doubt Cayito's betrayal. He knew the reasons well. Yes, sir, and this is the truth, every time he could say our troop was an example, he did. Even so, we never trusted him completely. Higinio respected whoever respected him, and that was right. You have to respect everybody. Now, if someone doesn't respect you, you tell him to go straight to hell. We didn't trust him from the day we learned he had been a bandit. That ended our doubts about him, but we didn't throw it in his face. He always behaved like a patriot. It's the same with whores and pimps and thieves. You think they're the worst there is, and it isn't true. The worst are the hypocrites.

We didn't see much fighting with Higinio. The only large battle was Arroyo Prieto. The rest was just passing the time. At Arroyo Prieto we fought for several hours and won.

It was a serious fight. We didn't have more than two or three casualties. Higinio acquitted himself well in the war. He quickly found the right way.

Higinio liked a little bit of fighting. A man who didn't fight was a man who had no say in matters. No sir. That kind of quiet war, two or three little shots scattered around was worse than a raging battle. Much worse!

There were only few times I got disgusted with the officers. With Higinio at El Vizcaíno I got a direct, personal order to report to Colonel Aranda as his aide. I didn't like that much. I went to Higinio immediately, and I told him clearly: "Look, I didn't come to the war to be anyone's aide. I'd be damned if I was going to be putting on someone's leggings and cleaning his boots!" Higinio stared me right in the eye and didn't say a word. He turned his back, and I beat it from his side in a hurry. The result was fifteen days of imaginaria. The imaginaria was a special guard duty. You had to spend the whole day on guard marching around the camp. If you were on imaginaria, you couldn't even sleep a wink. It was a living hell with the rain showers, the mud, the filth, the mosquitoes, well...If out of anger somebody didn't complete the imaginaria, they put him in the field stocks. It didn't matter you were going to fight, that you were going to risk your neck, they still punished you.

That Aranda fellow was the President of the Council of Veterans after the war. I seen him a lot. But he didn't remember me. He never said hello, anyhow. As I see it, he got into the war so the hanging tree wouldn't get him because he was a criminal. He killed his wife to take over her property. Aranda found another aide. They didn't come back to ask me about that kind of job again. Higinio and I never spoke again. I lost my horse, reins, saddle...they were given to Aranda's new aide. They left me stripped clean.

A few days later, Corojito, the one they named to be the aide, came through the camp cutting it up with the horse. He was nothing more than an ass-kissing mulatto. That made me mad, and one day I up and walked to the village of Jicotea. I had permission to look for food. I went with Juan Fábregas, who had been with me throughout the war. Juan and I agreed to raid the Spanish fort and capture two horses for ourselves. As we approached, we saw that there were dogs at the entrance and all along the fence. We took off our clothes so the bastards couldn't smell anything and put them in a little weighing scale close by. We had to get those horses so as not to finish the war on foot.

We snuck up little by little, and reaching the barbed wire, we saw the guard. Since we were dark and naked, he didn't seem to see us. We continued on and went in through the gate, creeping around the sentry box. The sentry was asleep. We grabbed two horses and took off bareback. We didn't even need candles. Lots of folks went thieving with candles to scare the dogs. I swear dogs are useless as guards. Geese, yes. If a fort had geese, no one would dare approach it. Geese were used a lot in private homes during Spanish rule, but now you don't see them any more.

When we got back to the camp, everyone was amazed, asked us: "Man, where did you come by those horses?" Juan said, "From the fort." No one said a word. They probably didn't believe him. That horse went through the rest of the war with me. I didn't give him a name, and I didn't take care of him like the first one. He was a pretty palomino, real pretty. At the Caracas mill, after the war, I got forty pesos for him.

I don't know what happened to Juan's horse. What I began to notice was that Juan started to be really short with him. He was no longer at ease. Juan changed from day to night. One day I realized he was missing. People came to me and said, "Hey, your buddy went over to the other side." I paid no attention. I thought he had gone out to hunt guinea pigs. The days passed, and I didn't see him around anywhere. Then I got word that he had surrendered to the Spanish. To tell the truth, that sent chills down my spine. Then I got mad. Anger and strength at the same time. I went on fighting in the war out of personal pride. I never seen Fábregas again. I looked for him at the end of the war, but I never found him.

A few weeks after Juan left, we went off in the direction of Santa Rosa, a big estate where there was a general headquarters. There Martín Morúa Delgado joined up with us. I seen him clear as day. He was very tall, a sort of light-skinned mulatto with brown hair. He didn't fight. He was a lieutenant without ever holding a machete in his hand. But he was book man. He spent his time in the headquarters' files. He arranged the shelves and ordered paper. He was one of those kinds of men. The war for him was done with words.

After some years passed, he became famous, and even provoked the rebellion of the blacks in Alto Songo. He was the smartest man who ever got to the Congress. And the greatest. Some whites said he was a partisan. Those whites were Americans. They accused him of being a partisan because of his race, because of the color of his skin.

The real partisans were backwoodsmen and stupid. Don't come to me with some story about a man of letters becoming a partisan. There was an equal number of whites as blacks who were partisans. That's true. There were partisans who were Spanish, Canary Islanders, and Cubans. I didn't know of any Chinese.

The partisans' tactics were different from the revolutionaries'. Fire shot out of their eyes. They were men who were full of venom, with rotting guts. When they saw a small group of Mambises they would fall on them to capture them. If they caught them, they killed them, that's all. The Spanish, who fought face to face, didn't kill like that, in cold blood. They had a different concept. I wouldn't say we fought like equals. They had ammunition, good saddles, reigns, spurs, the complete kit...We rode bareback. They supplied all those things to the partisans, so that's why they felt superior.

I never seen more hateful people. Even now, after all this time, there are still some on this island. Think of all the time gone by. Even so, they're still around, and they give you an evil look. I know one who spends his time playing a guitar. He's a potbellied, fat black man. Each time I go by him, he lowers his head and keeps on playing. I don't look at him to avoid trouble. But the day he starts any funny business, I'll give him a such a punch that he won't live to tell about it.

Before the war I knew lots of smart-asses, town toughs who lived by their wits. They were drifters and bums, and Saturdays and Sundays they fought and showed off and looked for trouble and got drunk...Almost all of those men, blacks and whites, were partisans. They didn't have any other way out. They knew the war was no tea party, and they were looking for the easy life. León was one of them. He was a scout for the partisans and had been the great friend, hand and glove, of Valentín the Executioner, who killed loads of people with the garrote. That's what the partisans were like. So anybody who tells me that Morúa was a partisan is a traitor and a liar.

When I set myself to thinking about those bastards, during the time people like me fought hunger, struggled knee-deep in mud and all that filth of the war, I feel an urge to string them up. The saddest thing is that Cubans never punished the partisans. Máximo Gómez himself wanted to make a deal. They say it was a political convenience. But to tell the truth, I'm not convinced that it was a matter of convenience. I would have put those men up against a wall like this Revolution did with the murderers of the previous government. A clean wall.

I can't bring myself to comprehend, I never did understand why Máximo Gómez said in the Quinta de los Molinos Park, when the war was over, that in Cuba there were no victors or vanquished. That was the phrase. I heard it because I was present at that speech. It didn't sit well with the troops. That meant that the partisans were made equal to the Spanish invaders. There were some who objected to that phrase.

Colonel Isidro Acea, who was as black as a Totí crow, got into his carriage and went to the demonstration after Gómez had said those words. He got there mad because he was a black man who didn't believe in anyone. He was a born fighter. He got his coach into the Quinta de los Molinos, and when people saw it was him they began to shout. It was said that it was the blacks who shouted. That's untrue. All the patriots there were yelling. Isidro got through the crowd saying, "Make way." And he came up to the front where Mario Menocal was. All the generals and the people had a healthy respect for him because he was brave and ferocious. He went up to Menocal, and said to him: "Those people who are outside there are going to come in here."

There were some iron bars that didn't allow free entry, and Acea was promising people they could enter. Menocal looked at him astounded and didn't answer. Máximo Gómez continued his speech. Acea raised his voice and said to Menocal: "What's going on, can the people get in or not? If they can't, I'll knock your head off." So Menocal had to give the order to let the people in. The riot was terrible. Everybody rushed for the platform. They carried Isidro Acea on their shoulders because he had humiliated the big brass. Máximo Gómez finished his speech, and no one paid any attention to him. That day he made a mistake with that little statement about "neither victors nor vanquished."

The partisans had to be eliminated. Thinking back on it again, Colonel Acea was a bit of a showoff. And since I have never liked the kind of men who bragged a lot, that day I swallowed Gomez' words, and I didn't turn against him. I thought what Isidro had done was too much. But in war you never know who's going to attack first. All the men who were listening to the speech were surprised by the Colonel's arrival. I remember the affair well because in those days I had just arrived in Havana with the troops. I had been in the capital something like a week. It was the first time I had ever been there. At first it seemed strange to me, then I got used to it, but I never liked it much really. I did like the countryside, and the woods especially.

In those days, with the war won, Havana was a carnival. Blacks had fun anyway they could. I was surprised by all the black people who lived there in Havana. Wherever you looked there was a black. The women came out into the streets with all the happiness and joy of the war's being ended. How can I tell all about it. I think I had more than fifty women in a week. Almost all the partisans' women got together with the liberators. One came up to me, and said: "I want you to take me with you, my husband was a partisan." I left that one behind because she was old. But each time a little silver fish crossed in front of me, I reached out my net and trapped it. I didn't even have to say a word. The women offered themselves to me ready. They saw you wearing the uniform of a liberator, with the machete, and it seems that's what they wanted.

Seeing that I'm not much of a party-goer, I wanted to take them off right away to the other fun and games. Many went straight to it. Others dragged me to the port district, where there was a fountain and a street with street lamps, and you could see cargo ships near by. Around there was more rumba than in any other place, both the rumba of cajón and kettle drum. They played on some tiny little cajoncitos and on drums they put between their legs. All the streets and inside the houses were filled with little leather stools. People would sit to watch, and old folks as well as young would go on dancing until they dropped. The ñáñigos' open patios were also lit up.

There were gunshots, knifings, drunken sprees, fights of all sorts. Those tahonas never ceased. Some folks who were dissatisfied with the way the Cubans governed themselves began to sing that thing about Santa Eulalia so it seemed like a prayer:

> Santa Eulalia's watching
> how Cubans runnin' gov'ment
> and it makes her so sad, so sad.
> Oh Lord, the Queen's abawlin'.

I was feeling happy. I never thought the war would come to an end. It was the same when I heard about Emancipation in the woods. Such things are not easy to believe. In the war I got used to going around naked, to seeing bayonets almost everyday and fleeing from the partisans. When they told me there was an Armistice, I didn't know what to say[19]. I didn't believe it. In Havana I became completely convinced. The world just seemed like it was going to come to an end. On the street they cheered Máximo Gómez and kissed his coat. There wasn't a single Cuban who didn't shout: "Viva Cuba libre!"

Complete strangers shook hands in the streets and threw their hats and kerchiefs in the air...I can't describe it well because I felt it so much. Those were moments of my own that I can't remember clearly. I remember the clothes, the hats better, the styles the Americans brought...They said men should go about bareheaded. Some folks did. That never sat well with me. I never take off my hat except to lie down to sleep. Your head ought to be properly covered always. In my opinion it shows a lack of respect to go around exhibiting your cranium. The Americans didn't give a hoot. Everything was ok with them. Above all with the tourists who were a bunch of thieves.

The capital had a strange feel about it. Things there were louder, more vulgar. For people new to the city, that's the best thing in the world. People went a little silly with all the distractions, with the drunkenness and such. I let loose among the women. But even with that and all, I stayed calm. I didn't get turned around. And after a few days you didn't know who you could trust. I was lodging in a wooden house that belonged to some acquaintances of mine. Some of the liberators slept in other folks' houses for a few days. The whole city opened its doors. Havana was a hospitable place during those years. But I wasn't taken in by all that business of street lamps and drinking and cheap women. I didn't like it, and that's one thing everyone knows about me. I thought the pimps were repulsive—bums who lived off the air and whatever they could steal Only in Havana. Because in other places they wouldn't have put up with those types.

In the countryside, laws are stricter, the laws of men who see things as they really are. Here in the city, the pimps had free reign. They strolled about, whistled, screwed around... They had the habit of wearing polo shirts monogrammed with the letters: HR. They were made of long lasting cotton. They wore good shoes, too, but they were ugly, deerskin or carpet. Many called them mules, which is a style from Spain.

Those scoundrels used to tie a red kerchief around their necks just to show off. They really beat up on the whores, knocking them about. That's the first thing I seen when I got off the train in this city: braggarts with stilettos, their shirttails tied around their waists, slapping around the street walkers. Those men never took a good look at themselves in the mirror. If they had, they might have stopped that craziness of shuffling around in those mules, beating on the whores. The Americans were the only ones who put a stop to the pimps. They sent them to who-knows-where outside of Havana, or they set them to breaking stones in the street. Those pimps swung the sledge hammer in the sun, with blisters on their backs, the sons of bitches!

Because of all that I didn't like it in the city. True, you had to know how life was here then. We, the liberators, found things new and strange, but the city folks probably would have said the countryside was hell. What hurt the most was how the Americans put us in a bind. It seems some people thought the Americans had come for pleasure. Later the opposite was clear, that they came to grab the best piece of pie for themselves. The people just let it happen. There were folks who were happy the Americans took the bull by the horns. And they said, as some still do today, that the best part of the war was the American intervention.

At that time, something happened with a priest that seemed to me to be the devil's work. That priest suffered the worst humiliation I have ever saw. The Americans said he was insolent, and they put him to breaking stones in downtown Havana, with his collar and all, in the street, over there where the Palacio de los Presidentes stands today.

All the old folks know about that. And they know the Americans were to blame. I went to see it because, by my mother's grave, I thought it was a lie. I got up early, and went running over to the small plaza where I had been told the priest was working. I seen him right away in the sun with his robes sticking to his body. Since priests are the most delicate of beings, I froze up. But it was him all right, in collar and robes. So there was no story or phantasma. The women who passed by and saw the priest would make a cross over their faces because they didn't believe it. I pinched myself on the arm to make sure. After that, you never heard another word about that priest. Personally, I think he must haunt the place, waiting for revenge.

The Americans didn't care much for the blacks. They called them "Nigger, nigger." And then they laughed. They kept right on pestering the blacks who paid any attention to them. The ones who didn't react were left alone. They never messed with me. Fact is that I never could stand them. I never went drinking with any of them. Whenever I could, I kept my distance. When the war ended, the talk started about whether the blacks had fought or not. I know that ninety-five percent of the blacks fought in the war. Then the Americans began to say it was only seventy-five percent. Well, no one criticized those statements. The blacks ended up out in the street as a result. Brave men thrown like savages into the streets. That was wrong, but that's what happened.

Not even one percent of the police force were blacks because the Americans claimed that when a black gets power, when he's educated, it hurts the white race. So then they separated the blacks completely. White Cubans kept quiet, they didn't do a thing, and that's how it was until nowadays. It's different now because I seen white men with black women, and blacks with white women, which is more touchy, on the street, in the cafes, everywhere.

Morúa and Campos Marquetti[20] tried to straighten out the problem, and they gave some government jobs to blacks. Positions as night watchmen, doormen, mailmen...Even so, when the army was disbanded, the black revolutionaries were unable to remain in the city. They returned to the country, to the cane fields, tobacco fields, to whatever, except to the offices. The partisans had more opportunities, even being traitors and all. That's the plain truth of it. General Maceo himself would have had to have hung a lot of people in the woods to have controlled the situation.

Later everyone said the Americans were the most rotten of all. And I agree, they were the rottenest. But you have to remember that the white Cubans were just as much to blame as the Americans because they let themselves be ordered around in their own country. All of them, from the Colonels to the janitors. Why didn't the people rebel over the Maine incident? Don't believe any cock and bull stories, either. Even the littlest kid knew the Americans blew the Maine up themselves to get into the war. If the people had gotten riled up then, everything would have been different. A lot of things wouldn't have happened. But when the hour of truth came, no one said one word or did a single thing. Máximo Gómez, who I thought knew something, clammed up and died with the secret. I believe this with all my heart, and may I drop dead if I'm lying.

Back then, I knew more things, more of the dirty tricks which history has covered up. I discussed them only with my friends. Now things have gotten all mixed up in my head. In spite of that, I can remember the most important things, though I can count on the fingers of two hands the times I've spoken of them with anyone. One time I started to say that the story of the American intervention in Santiago de Cuba was poppycock—that they couldn't have taken the town by themselves. Well, there were some who argued with me about that so as to not to become implicated. The good thing about all this is that now you can talk about it. And the truth is that in Santiago the one who really fought was Calixto García. The Americans bombed the sector where the Spaniard called Vara del Rey was in command. But Calixto García attacked Vara del Rey's troops by land and defeated them.

Then the Americans raised the flag to let it be known they had taken the city. That was a terrible mess. Vara del Rey, with five hundred men, slaughtered a whole bunch of Americans. The worst of it was that the American commander gave the order to bar Cubans from entering the city. That brought things to the boiling point. When the Cubans weren't allowed into town, they got furious with the Americans, and Calixto García had a few hard words with them. To tell the truth, I prefer the Spaniard to the American, but the Spaniard in his own country. Everyone in his own country. Today I don't like the American, even on his own territory.

In the war, Spaniards said to the women: "Hey Pancha, your ol' dad is shooting at me but bloody damn, he eats the food anyway." They weren't as savage as the Americans. The thing with the Americans was absolutely the limit. They dug a hole and threw the food in it. All the people knew about that, they lived through it. Wood, Theodore Roosevelt, the other one, I can't even remember now what his name was, the whole bunch of degenerates who sank this country.

In Cienfuegos,[21] about the year eighteen hundred and ninety nine, a group of Mambises had to wave our machetes in the air at a few American soldiers, scoundrels who wanted to have all the criollas like they were meat in the market. I don't think they even respected their own mothers. They would approach the houses, see a pretty woman in the window or in the doorway, go up to her, and say "Fucky, Fucky, Margarita," and in they would go. I saw all that in Cienfuegos. With that business of "fucky, fucky," they made a screaming mess. We found out about it and went over there to keep an eye out. They were dressed in khaki, pressed and neat, but almost always drunk. Claudio Sarría, who had been a sergeant, gave the order to raise the machete. And we went over there like wild beasts.

We were on the lookout, and, sure enough, a little bunch of them began to cause trouble on a street near the docks. They were fooling around with the women, patting their behinds and laughing. I never got so hot under the collar during the war as on that day. We fell on them with bare machetes and chased them out of there. Some took off for the docks where their ship was to hide. Some shot up into the hills of Escambray like rockets. They never bothered any of the woman around there again.

When the Americans went out, they would go with an officer and enter a cafe like school boys. I've never forgotten that day because all of us who took part in that incident were risking our necks. Anyway, the Americans did worse things later on, and nobody's said a peep.

The Americans took Cuba by trickery. It's true that we can't blame them for everything. The really guilty ones were the Cubans who obeyed their orders. There's a great deal there to investigate there. I'm sure that when all of these deceptions that are now hidden are uncovered that the world will come to an end. But it has to come to an end because right now the Americans have their hand in everywhere they want.

When the war was over those little Cuban Colonels gave McKinley free reign so he could do whatever he wanted with this island. Some of the Marqués de Santa Lucías' properties were over there where the Santa María sugarmill is. As I later found out, he left that land to the revolutionaries. What happened was that the Americans split it with Menocal. The dirtiest deal of the whole war!

Menocal didn't say a word; he just took over. He was more American than McKinley himself. That's why nobody ever liked him. He was a business patriot not a jungle fighter.

And a million other things like that without an end in sight. Back then I used to think about things more, but then I'd get heated up and have to rub my head. I'm still a little thoughtful at times. But I don't think about these things for fun. The thoughts just come to me, and it would take an earthquake to knock them out of my head.

What has saved me the most is that I've kept quiet because you can't trust anyone. The man who trusts too much will drown alone. When the war ended and all the troops returned to Havana, I began to watch folks. Many wanted the soft and comfortable life of the city. Well, those who stayed came out worse than if they had gone back to the forest. Worse, because the pushing and shoving began, the cheating and the lies. "Man, are you going to get rich here!" And shit! He was the first to die of hunger. That's why when the leaders said: "The war is over, you have to go to work," I picked up my pack and went to the train station close to the Havana Wall. I still haven't forgotten it. Then and there I shipped out to Las Villas. I asked for a ticket to that place. Las Villas is the best place there is in Cuba, and since I was born there...

The partisan soldiers were put in offices because they were businessmen, or some such nonsense like that, or they had a pretty daughter, or money. I returned to the countryside without a peso in my pocket. I gave myself a temporary discharge.

When I arrived at Remedios I met some acquaintances of mine. Then I left for Cruces and began to work in the San Agustín Maguaraya sugarmill. At my same old job. It seemed like I was back in the past all over again. I started working on the conveyor belt. Later I went to the mixer where you were more comfortable, and you earned thirty-six pesos a month. I lived alone in thatch barracoon until I felt the urge to have a woman. Well, I kept one, too, for a little while until things got difficult. Then I let her go and went back to living alone.

I didn't make any friends in Maguararya. I've never liked troublemakers and slobs. There was no one there who was friendly with me. It's also true that I never was much of a carouser. Everybody goes to market with their own basket.

I worked all day long, and when night came I went home to rest and to pull off the chiggers, the most painful bugs in the world. I went around in almost all the villages in Las Villas. I was an auctioneer, a nightwatchman, the last straw! I learned all the trades so that no one could get the better of me.

I got to Havana one day when Máximo Gómez had already died. When a man dies people quickly forget him.

The only thing I heard was that he appeared every now and then in the Quinta de los Molinos Park, and that there was a witch in the park.

I went through a park and saw that he had been mounted up on a bronze horse. I went on, and about a half a mile down, they had Maceo mounted on a horse just like it. The difference was that Gómez faced the North, and Maceo the town and the people.

Everybody should pay attention to that. It's all there. And I'll keep on saying it as long as I live because you shouldn't silence the truth. And though I may die tomorrow, I wouldn't give up my sense of honor for anything. If I could, I would tell the whole story now, all of it. Because back then, when you were dirty and naked in the hills, you could see those crisp, clean Spanish soldiers with the best weapons. And you had to keep quiet. That's why I say I don't want to die so that I can fight all the battles yet to come. I won't get into the trenches or use any of these modern weapons. A machete will do for me.

Afterword:
TESTIMONIAL NARRATIVE

The Alchemy of Memory

When I used to look at the walls of the colonial forts in Havana and the cathedrals with their resounding towers, I would think about the arms that had erected those monuments stone by stone being worn away by sweat and fevers. I listened to the stories my father told me about the exploits of captains and governors and I thought about the hidden efforts, about the collective daring of those who had remained behind the invisible walls of history. I was a different kind of child. For me the epic of events was interesting when it was colored by that hidden gesture, by the quiet rumble of those who in the grip of sacrifice truly made the history of every day. Those ghosts couldn't make it into the travel books or into the tales of the enthusiastic chroniclers. First because they were everywhere and also because they were invisible in the eyes of the crafty ruler. The rich trove of legends, myths and sayings created by the so-called "people with no history" remained anonymous. It would wait for a vindicating age, a will to evolve and a foundation to be laid, which on the strength of testimony, like a faithful compensation, would give back to them the light with which they had forged the ill-fated days of emperors and princes. The lessons of Latin American history in the '60s give a devastating impulse to works of testimony. I believe the Cuban Revolution, with its powerful organic influence, provided all the literature of this type that developed in the Americas with a rejuvenating nutrient. The insertion of history into the new narrative, working like a compass and a walking stick, has meant as much for subjectivism as for testimonial realism, the two tendencies that go linked together in a single strategy that incites and provokes new ideological trails. The designation "testimonial novel" constitutes an attempt to differentiate between its form and other possible forms of testimony and of novel, some shoddy and some deviant.

Testimonial novel, in this sintagmatic definition, implies a conjunction of styles, a coming together of approaches and a fusion of objectives, a confrontation with problems within the American context: violence, dependency, neocolonialism, the falsification of history by means of schematisms, applied and reapplied. The testimonial novel critically examines not only ethnic, cultural and social stereotypes, it also reworks several traditional concepts of literature: realism, autobiography, the relationship between fiction and history. History will always appear through the significant, individual moments of marginalized persons. Testimonial literature will revise a mangled, deformed interpretation of the past to offer a vision from the perspective of the class struggle. Intentionality constitutes the very fabric of this kind of work. It looks at the marginalized, and quasi marginalized people from the widest perspective, scrutinizing all the angles, without falling into formalisms plagued by demagogic and pseudomarxist intentions.

The advent of the Cuban Revolution brought about a violent subversion of traditional bourgeois values. It was the greatest and most devastating experience of my life. With a brush stroke we became the spokesmen of an all-knowing view of the world and of our role in the life of our country. If the period prior to the entry of Fidel Castro in Havana had been tedious and anxiety-provoking, what followed was a time of excitement and jubilation. Identity, our most intimate subject matter, so obscure and amorphous for other countries, was revealed in all its potency in the pristine years of my training as a writer and ethnologist. Studies of traditional popular culture became necessary in order to understand ourselves more fully. And the search for the poetry of engagement carried us to a new and commanding insistence on our national identity. Aristotle, with clairvoyant judgment, said that poetry can at times be more scientific than history. For me that has been demonstrated in fact. I understand literary vocation in its communicative function to be intricately entwined with the roots of concrete culture, of a Latin American culture in my case. I am a Latin American to the extent that I am Cuban. If my work has taken on some resonance it is due to the fact that I have tried to present an image of my country in all its powerful authenticity, stripped of provincial folklore.

I am not a pure writer but something like the cross between a falcon and a tortoise. I have tried to bring together sociological-anthropological interests and the literary, convinced that they travel together in underground caverns, seeking each other out and nourishing each other in joyful reciprocity. If I move back and forth between these disciplines it's because I believe it's time they join hands without denying each other.

Memory, as part of the imagination, has been a touchstone in my books. Thanks, many thanks, noble and heavenly Mnemosyne. I aspire to be a sounding board for the collective memory of my country. For that purpose I resort to oral discourse, to myths and to the anthropomorphic Cuban fable: a subject whose purest expression was elaborated by Alejo Carpentier in *The Kingdom of This World*. I don't aspire to make categorical definitions, nor do I offer solutions to social problems, which are the proper obligation of the politicians. The only desire I have is to reveal the human heart, the heart of the men that traditional historiography has marked with the sign of a proverbial fatalism by writing them off as "people without a history." I think I have indeed shown that the life of men of the so-called culture of poverty as defined by Oscar Lewis, doesn't always lack the will to exist, or lack a consciousness of history. And even when such a life is anchored in a sense of marginality the flame of that life glows toward the future.

I no longer believe in genres, as the people have never believed in them. The people sang ballads, and rhymed couplets, used theatrical and narrated forms, and subordinated all of that to the effectiveness of the message, and the people never got stuck on one thing. I think our peoples still have much to tell in their own tongue, not in one invented for them to undermine them.

The ability of the gestor of the testimonial novel to balance telling stories in that tongue and not adulterate its idiosyncratic essence is testimonial's necessary mechanism, the sine qua non of its existence. That equilibrium isn't achieved with a microphone or with the mistaken use of computers. It is only attained by sharpening the ability to hear the intonations and the music of history, to hear the most guarded, introspective form of oral discourse. It is a nourishment needed retroactively at this level of communication in order to achieve the real understanding of identity. I think that in language lies the key to this knowledge and for this strategy. All lives are important but one has to know how to extract from them the tone of their universal resonance.

When it rescues people's pride in being alive, and when it vindicates the values that were most concealed and reveal the true identity of the people in society, then the testimonial novel has made contributions to knowledge and to the adaptation of the collective psyche to the idea of what it means to be Cuban and what it means to be Latin American, to the idea of authenticity, to the true and the essential.

The images and the characters put into motion in the genre of the testimonial novel try to show the ethnological aspects of history, to show the social process, its internal dynamics. They try to examine individual cases under the control of patterns of group conduct and to supply effective, impartial markers for the interpretation of history and not its description in coarse detail, which has been the usual practice of textbooks taken from ancient, moth infested archives or that come from the tendentious thinking of men of the past.

The testimonial novel should in no way be the story of an atypical or sensational character, or of a pleasing or adventurous type who provides the reader with a superfluous source of pleasure or diversion. It has to be something more than that. It should represent the world in reverse. The function of the testimonial novel as rescuer of a foundational language, as a rescuer of the old historical novel, should be to give back the original sound of storytelling to the contemporary novel. It should be interpreted as the burgeoning of a new cultural language, in battle with a real deceit that is propped up by long-standing clichés.

We know that Art is impure and its nature is protean, so we should try to seek out its most translucid depths. Art's greatest mission is that we find ourselves there. I want to be just one of the bellows in the sounding box of my people. Let the people, for whom I write, recognize themselves in my voice, and discover there that their demons are pacified in the substance of time. It is a great and ambitious task.

Memorialist, historian, story-teller, anything but a falsifier of the history of the people who couldn't tell their story, to whom I offer myself in caring and ready servitude. I want to here salute the Brothers Grimm, the evanescent witches who flew from the Canary Islands to Cuba, with potash spread under their arms, Changó of the land of Oyó, Queztalcoatl, and Tezcatlipolca, called the "great tree of mirrors," and the entire holy *Santa Compaña* of Galicia. Because I know that they are all the poetic symbol of the culture that has given us a tongue with which to tell our stories. Latin American culture today spreads its leaves all around, the leaves of a great mythological tree, all over the lands of the world.

Miguel Barnet

Footnotes

1 It was common in the Spanish Colony for Negro slaves to use the name of their country of origin as a surname after their given name.

2 Don Honorato Bertrand Chateausalins seems to have been, in 1831, the first author to recommend their construction. In the *El Vademécum de los Hacendados Cubanos*, he gives the advice that the slave's quarters "be built in the shape of a barracoon with a single door, for which the administrator or overseer takes care to collect the keys at night. Each room to be built should have no other entrance than a single door with a small barred window beside it so the Negro cannot communicate with others at night."

3 Moreno Fraginals, Manuel, *El ingenio. El Complejo Económico Social Cubano de Azúcar*. La Habana: Comisión Nacional Cubana de la UNESCO. Tomo I (1760-1860), pages 163 and 164. "Marking the rhythm of the interminable chores, the bell was like a great religious and profane symbol of the mill. In the same way that it is hard to conceive of a church without a bell tower, so there was no mill or coffee plantation without a bell. The bell ringer of the mill did not need to learn varied or complex patterns of urban life and it was generally an old black who was no good for tasks of production, incapacitated psychologically for running away, who lived next to the bell, his daily death. Above the nearby fields of Trinidad, the tower of the Manacas mill still stands, full of legend. On the very top the empty niche remains where the bell once hung. The tower—lookout, fort and bell—is the symbol of slave labor in the cane fields. There the bell signaled daily, 16, 18 or 20 hours of work per day. And also serving as communication throughout the wide valley, since there was a chime to call the ox driver, another for the administrator, another for the overseer, and sometimes even a small flourish announced that a slave had left for the mill's cemetery."

4 Madden, Richard R., *La isla de Cuba*. Habana, Consejo Nacional de Cultura, 1964, p. 142. Madden writes about "mills where during the period of cutting the cane and crushing, the work day lasted twenty continuous hours, frequently for more than six months a year, and rarely or never for less than five, since the prevailing opinion on this subject,

generally practiced by the masters, is that 4 hours of sleep for a slave is sufficient."

5 James Steele, in his *Cuban Sketches*, describes cases of pregnant black women who were ordered to receive a heavy whipping on the belly. Bernardo Chateausalins, speaking about the female slave, says that many had miscarriages because they were made to cut 400 arrobas [5 tons (sic)] of cane on a daily basis in their ninth month of pregnancy.

6 Moreno Fraginals, Manuel, *op. cit.*, p. 156. "...Sexual life at the mill was limited for many reasons and the primary one being the great imbalance between the sexes. The sugar mill owners imported males exclusively and there were very few plantations that had women. In the logic of plantation economics at the beginning of the XIXth century, it made no sense to purchase women slaves since they were considered livestock of low productive yield. It was unprofitable to bring them in numbers because the production did not give return on the investment. Brought in small groups, they were the focus of continuous strife among the black men. Some plantation owners tried to offer a religious excuse for this imbalance and asserted that they didn't bring women in order to avoid the sin of sexual contact between persons who were not married. In reply to that argument, Father Caballero gave a precise answer: 'A worse sin would have been if they were all masturbators, evil doers and sodomites!'"

7 Juan Marinello, a Cuban writer who has distinguished himself through his essays and books on José Martí.

8 Núñez Jiménez, Antonio, "La Gesta Libertadora." Revista *INRA*. Año II, No. 8, pp. 22-25. "The oppressed, always at some initial disadvantage, bent nature to their favor during the 'knights' competitions. The sparse mountains, the lush forests and the dark caverns were the allies of the fighters against oppression. Many times the slaves sought refuge in the hills living hidden among the rocks and protected by the density of the woods. The fugitive runaways who obeyed individual impulses of freedom quickly became groups organized to resist the owners. The palenques were born, formed by groups of blacks who once lived along the steep hillsides or in the remote caves."

In the *Memorias de la Real Sociedad Patriótica de la Habana*, published in 1839, in the article on the caves of Cubitas, in Camagüey, we read: "Among the many rarities worthy of admiration which Nature gave to Cubitas is the great cave or the cave of the runaway slaves. The big cave is found half a league from the northern point of the Estrada district, to the right on the road that leads to Guanajá. It is below the incline of Toabaquei and the flat land, at the same time. You enter through an opening that seems like a bread oven and descend to the depths along a thick jagüey root... Formerly, this cave served as the hideout for runaway slaves, but they have abandoned it. The means by which the runaways were obliged to evacuate the cave was to gather many branches and hot pepper and burn them at the entrance, so that it made a lot of smoke. That operation was sufficient cause, so that on seeing themselves on the verge of dying of suffocation, they should leave and turn themselves in at their discretion."

[9] Arsenio Martínez Campos, Captain General of the Island of Cuba. He was the head of the Spanish army in 1868 during the Ten Years' War. He remained in Cuba until 1878 when the end of the war was declared in the Zanjón Pact.

[10] Moreno Fraginals, Manuel, *op. cit.*, p. 166. "...sleep was one of the most serious problems at the mill. Especially in those places that maintained the idea that the blacks could stand 20 hours of daily work and put men who had spent 10 hours cutting and hoisting cane in the sun to work at night in the boiler room. They gave the inoffensive name of *faena* or chores to those tasks. Some mills required their slaves to carry out *faenas* and *contrafaenas*. A black who completed his normal work, his *faena* and *contrafaena* employed some 22 hours in that labor. As a reward he was allowed to sleep 6 hours the next day and then went back to the same workday of 20 to 22 hours."

[11] Manuel Salamanca y Negrete, Captain General of the Island of Cuba from March, 1889 to February, 1890.

[12] Cayito Alvarez, a colonel in the Army of Liberation. In the War of Independence he fought under the command of General Antonio Maceo, who named him the responsible party, with Bermúdez and others, in several cases of wrongdoing. Bermúdez, who got to be a brigadier general, was condemned to death and executed.

[13] Martí lived in New York, not Tampa. But in Cayo Hueso and Tampa there was a large Cuban immigrant community, organized by Martí, that decidedly supported him in his struggle for Cuban Independence.

14 Martínez Fortún y Foyo, José A. *Cronología Remediana*, Remedios, 1937. This pamphlet reports the kidnapping of Don Modesto Ruíz and gives 1889 as the date of incident.

15 This does not refer to General Vicente García who became President of the (unofficial) Republic at the end of the Ten Years' War.

16 Carlos Manuel de Céspedes, a notable revolutionary who initiated the Ten Years' War. He was declared to be the Father of the Nation.

17 Higinio Esquerra Rodríguez. He disembarked in Las Villas with expeditionary forces on the 25th of July, 1895. He got to be a brigadier general.

18 The shout that announced the beginning of the War of Independence. It took place in the town of Baire the 24th of February, 1895.

19 The cease-fire was established in 1898.

20 Generoso Campos Marquetti, Liberal Party representative in the House in 1912. He seconded Martín Morúa Delgado's resolution to ban racist political parties in Cuba.

21 Rousseau y Díaz de Villegas, Pablo L., *Memoria Descriptiva, Histórica y Biográfica de Cienfuegos*. Cienfuegos, p. 269. A partial version of the incident: "On the 24th of June at four o'clock in the afternoon, when activity in the city was at its peak as a result of the celebration of the feast of San Juan, under the newly established government, three soldiers employed in the American Army's Office of the Commissioner of War, instigated a scene in a house of prostitution located at the far western end of Santa Clara street. The municipal police were attempting to arrest the instigators when Captain Fentón, who happened to be passing the place at that very moment, stopped his carriage and, in spite of police opposition, made the aforementioned soldiers get in and then quickly began to pull away.

"At that moment one of the soldiers inside the carriage fired at a policeman, who was trying to stop the vehicle's driver. Said policeman fell to the ground, shot to death by his aggressor. While that occurred, a detachment of American soldiers who had just arrived by rail, abandoned its custody of Cuban soldiers and began firing at the police, who were crouching behind the fence at the location in question, and killed an inhabitant of the neighborhood, Mr. Pablo Santa María, who was passing in a carriage along the Paso de Arango, with his three children. Order was restored a short time after the incident began, which in addition, left several different individuals wounded on account of the intervention of the Mayor of the city and General Esquerra, Chief of the Rural Guard, who directed themselves to the place where the American soldiers were firing, and, risking their lives, urged them to stop discharging their weapons.

"The facts here related caused a general protest against the conduct of the instigators of these conflicts."

("I comment on this event, which is here related in a partial version, because of its historical importance, since as far as I know it was the first armed encounter between Cubans and North Americans in response to the insolent, shameless conduct of the latter."—M. Barnet)

Glossary

alafia: An expression particularly used in fortune-telling with coconuts among the Lucumí to indicate that things are going well.

bagazo: bagasse, the remains of the cane, after crushing

batey: the sugarmill grounds, compound

besanas: an old agrarian measure

bozal, bozales: first generation Africans, who didn't speak Spanish well, hence the added notion of "simple minded"

Cabildo: an administrative council of inhabitants of a neighborhood, a town, a district. Among the Africans, tribal customs and practices were maintained.

cajón, cajoncito: boxes of different sizes used as drums

cachimbo: small sugarmill

Carabalís: ethnic group from the Guinea Coast who practiced the Calabar religion

caringa: a dance of African origin, popular in Las Villas province, no longer in use

calalú: Yoruba food, favorite of Changó, made with corn meal and pork

cazuela: a clay casserole pot, where ritual objects were put to create magic during ritual ceremonies

Changó: Yoruba god of thunder and lightning, love, virility, and music, associated with Saint Barbara

cimarrón: a runaway slave

Congo: African from the Congo or descendent of Congolese; related to them.

criollitos, criollos: like Creole, this is a term for a person of European descent born in the Americas. It is here also applied to the children born in slavery and, thus, to Africans born in Cuba, which is a special usage.

danza: a popular dance

danzón, danzones: the national dance of Cuba. A slow type of elegant dance

Eleggua: Yoruba god of roads, directions.

faina or faena: the overtime "chores" after the standard workday of twenty plus hours in the high season

Gangás: ethnic group, probably of sudanese origination

guajiro: white, country folk; hillbilly

guarapo: the raw cane juice

güijes: little river sprites or demons

Lucumí: a popular term in Cuba for an African from Nigeria and other Sudanese regions, mostly from the Gulf of Guinea

Mambises or Mambí: the Cuban Revolutionary troops

Mandingo: ethnic group from western Sudan

maní: a dance and/or game of severe physical conditions

mayombe: a bad spirit; one of the sects of the Regla de palo. To play mayombe meant to work magic for some utilitarian purpose.

Masungo: ethnic group of Bantu origin

ñáñigo: members of the Abakuá sect, for men only

Obatalá: Yoruba god of Creation

Ochún: Yoruba god of gold and sexuality

palenque: mountain hideout for fugitives

palero: a practitioner of the Congo rites of the Regla de palo.

palo: a ritual stick or object

Partido: jurisdiction overseen by a circuit judge

prenda: a Congo ritual object, receptacle for magical powers of the Regla de palo

quimbumbia: A Congo game and dance

raspadura: flavored molasses

regla: Regla de palo, magic spell to achieve some benefit

tahonas: rumba clubs in Havana

trapiches: sugar extraction machine and, by extension, the entire mill operation

vajajá: red-checked kercchief made in Boyajá in Haiti

voluntarios: Spanish Army auxiliaries made up of Spaniards living in Cuba

Yemayá: Yoruba goddess of the ocean and maternity

zapateo: a tapping or stomping dance common among white peasants

Curbstone Press, Inc.
is a non-profit publishing house dedicated to literature that reflects a
commitment to social change, with an emphasis on contemporary
writing from Latin America and Latino communities in the United
States. Curbstone presents writers who give voice to the unheard in a
language that goes beyond denunciation to celebrate, honor and teach.
Curbstone builds bridges between its writers and the public – from
inner-city to rural areas, colleges to community centers, children to
adults. Curbstone seeks out the highest aesthetic expression of the
dedication to human rights and intercultural understanding: poetry,
testimonials, novels, stories, photography.

This mission requires more than just producing books. It requires
ensuring that as many people as possible know about these books and
read them. To achieve this, a large portion of Curbstone's schedule is
dedicated to arranging tours and programs for its authors, working
with public school and university teachers to enrich curricula, reaching
out to underserved audiences by donating books and conducting
readings and community programs, and promoting discussion in the
media. It is only through these combined efforts that literature can truly
make a difference.

Curbstone Press, like all non-profit presses, depends on the support of
individuals, foundations, and government agencies to bring you, the
reader, works of literary merit and social significance which might not
find a place in profit-driven publishing channels. Our sincere thanks to
the many individuals who support this endeavor and to the following
foundations and government agencies: ADCO Foundation, J. Walton
Bissell Foundation, Inc., Witter Bynner Foundation for Poetry, Inc.,
Connecticut Commission on the Arts, Connecticut Arts Endowment
Fund, Lannan Foundation, LEF Foundation, Lila Wallace-Reader's
Digest Fund, The Andrew W. Mellon Foundation, National
Endowment for the Arts, and The Plumsock Fund.

Please support Curbstone's efforts to present the diverse voices and
views that make our culture richer. Tax-deductible donations can be
made to Curbstone Press, 321 Jackson Street, Willimantic, Connecticut
06226. Telephone: (203) 423-5110.